PRICE $ 7.50

Affairs of the Harp

Samuel O Pratt

Charles Colin   315 West 53rd Street New York 19, N.Y.

© Copyright 1964
CHARLES COLIN
New York 19, N. Y.

International Copyright Secured   Made in U.S.A.
All Rights Reserved, Including Public Performance for Profit

No part of this book may be reproduced in any form without permission in writing from the publisher.

Any arrangement or adaptation of the copyrighted compositions in this book without the permission of the copyright owner is an infringement of copyright.

Affairs of the Harp

being

An explanation of its maintenance and repair

and

A discussion of its Literature, Technique

and

Philosophy

for

The Performer, Teacher, Composer, Conductor and Critic

by

Samuel O. Pratt

© Copyright **1964** by Charles Colin, 315 West 53rd Street, New York 19, N. Y.
All Rights Reserved   International Copyright Secured   Made in U.S.A.

HARPOONS

by

Don Bluth

**Captions and other illustrations
by the author.**

To

Caroline Gardiner,
whose years of long suffering and faithful service are deeply appreciated, and whose quiet and unsung service to the harp world is hereby gratefully acknowledged.

TABLE OF CONTENTS

1.	INTRODUCTION	1
2.	HISTORY	5
3.	HOW THE HARP IS MADE	11
4.	HARPISTS, LITERATURE AND TECHNIQUE OF THE PAST	17
5.	THE ORCHESTRAL HARPIST	34
6.	ON THE QUALITY OF HARP MUSIC	42
7.	GLISSANDOS AND HARMONICS	46
8.	ON TEACHERS AND TEACHING	49
9.	FOUNDATION TO EXCELLENT TECHNIQUE	55
10.	FOR COMPOSERS	60
11.	TO MUSIC CRITICS	64
12.	FOR THE CONDUCTOR	69
13.	STRINGING	75
14.	TROUBADOUR TROUBLES	86
15.	WRAPPING THE PEDALS	89
16.	TUNING	94
17.	REGULATING THE ACTION	100
18.	BUZZES AND RATTLES	114
19.	BROKEN SPRINGS	119
20.	BROKEN PEDAL RODS	125
21.	TUNING PIN TROUBLES	130

22.	FROZEN PEDALS	133
23.	CLICKS AND CLACKS	137
24.	REMOVING THE ACTION	142
25.	SQUEAKS AND KAHOOCHES	145
26.	OIL IT RIGHT!	148
27.	THE BASE AND FEET	151
28.	NECKS - TWISTED AND BROKEN	156
29.	SOUND-BOARDS	160
30.	THE BODY AND THE BASE-BOARD	168
31.	COLUMNS AND CROWNS	172
32.	BENCHES AND STANDS	174
33.	OF WOOD AND GLUE	177
34.	THE FINISH - PRESERVING AND REPAIRING	180
35.	ANTIQUE HARPS	185
36.	STORING AND SHIPPING YOUR HARP	190
37.	DAMAGE AND INSURANCE	193
	BIBLIOGRAPHY	196
	ABOUT THE AUTHOR	197
	HARP COMPOSITIONS BY THE AUTHOR	200
	INDEX	202

LIST OF ILLUSTRATIONS

The harp has evolved . . .   4
A form of the Egyptian style of harp . . .   6
The harp has always had an aura of mystery . . .   8
The harp has five major parts . . .   10
Ninety-five percent of the harps made since 1889 . .   14
The great harpists of the past have nearly always
   been men . . .   16
In all ages and in all countries . . .   25
Most large orchestras employ both a first and
   second harp . . .   34
Make friends with the men who move and care
   for your harp . . .   38
Even though they seem to have a small tone,
   some harps . . .   41
Do not expect good practice unless . . .   48
The harp is a demanding instrument . . .   54
Harp festivals of the recent past . . .   59
The harp world today tends to be dominated
   by women . . .   63
The harp is a versatile and useful instrument . . .   68
Restringing is not a difficult task . . .   74
Some harpists sacrifice appearance . . .   77

Don't wind heavy strings too many times . . .	79
The tie knot . . .	79
How to allow slack in wire strings . . .	81
The wire strings should be inserted . . .	83
The Troubadour harp is virtually worry-free . . .	85
How to invert a harp to put on pedal felts . . .	88
How to wrap the pedal felts . . .	90
Intonation is never a problem on the harp . . .	93
Method for correcting the position of a disc . . .	103
Detail of Action, disc, links, arms, adj. nuts . .	107
A loose screw may cause a slight buzz . . .	113
Detail of knee-block, back-plate, back-plate screws	117
Detail of pedal assembly . . .	121
When replacing a rod, tie the harp securely . . .	124
Tuning pins rarely cause trouble . . .	129
A frozen pedal means a frozen action . . .	132
Clicks and clacks may mean a major operation . .	136
Detail of main action . . .	140
Detail of column and action . . .	147
Does your harp base need attention? . . .	150
A broken neck is easily diagnosed . . .	155
A vertical crack in the sound-board may be only a check . . .	163
The harp today is moving ahead . . .	171
Harpists tend to seek each other out . . .	176

A good cover will provide some protection . . .   182
Some harpists maintain that they have the
  world's greatest harp . . .   185
The harp trunk provides excellent protection . . .   189
A severe fall may cause hidden damage . . .   192
The style 30, Princess Louise . . .   195

CHAPTER ONE: INTRODUCTION

We hope by means of this little volume to help fill an almost complete vacuum in literature regarding the harp. As far as we know, this is the first book to deal with the repair and maintenance of the harp in any detail. There have been few books written on the harp at any period of history, and these have dealt almost exclusively with the personalities of its players and the evolution of the instrument only up to Erard. We have dealt only slightly with the personalities, and but a little more with their musical product. Our opinions are expressed at some length on many of the various subjects of interest primarily to the harpist. We have, for the sake of the harpist, indicated certain sections for the composer, critic and conductor. Taken alone, these sections would not add much to the understanding of these important people, so we strongly suggest that they read the rest of the book also, perhaps omitting only the sections detailing repairs and maintenance.

Our views have not been arrived at lightly, but over a period of many years of intimate association not only with the harp, but also with some of the greatest players and exponents of the instrument. Gleaning a bit from this one and that one has, we feel, given us a vantage point unobscured by utter devotion to any one master or school of playing. Constant contact with the performing musical world has also made us keep the harp in perspective as it fits into the concert and solo recital scene.

This book began as a series of notes prepared for lectures on the care and maintenance of the harp to be delivered at the Eastman School of Music in Rochester, New York and the Salzedo Harp Colony in Camden, Maine.

© Copyright **1964** by Charles Colin, 315 West 53rd Street, New York 19, N. Y.
All Rights Reserved   International Copyright Secured   Made in U S. A.

Our gratitude is hereby expressed to Miss Eileen Malone of Eastman and Miss Alice Chalifoux of Camden for that initial invitation, since repeated many times, and for the part that they thus played in the genesis of this work.

Further gratitude must also be expressed by the author to the late Carlos Salzedo for years of friendship and association with stimulating differences and agreements of opinion, and to Marcel Grandjany, whose undisputed rank as a leader of the harp world today and whose superb musicianship have been a source of inspiration and direction.

Thanks in great measure goes to Donald Bluth whose delightfully ironic and illuminating "Harpoons" grace the pages of this book and help enliven what might otherwise be a dull tome.

Much interesting and highly valuable harpistic information has been brought to light by the research of William Trezise who ran down the facts on many of our nebulous ideas and fuzzy recollections, and it is to be hoped that much of his research into the history of the harp, harpists and harp music will soon see the light of print. Our gratitude is hereby extended to him, also.

The latter part of this volume is intended to be a practical guide to the care and repair of the harp. It will attempt to outline what you can do to keep it operating and provide some information on what major repairs are possible and when they are necessary. Along the way we will touch on the construction and theory of the harp and perhaps take a timorous glance into the possible evolutionary history of the instrument.

In several cases we will be providing information not

so much for the harpist as for a qualified cabinet maker or machinist who may be able to perform major repairs for harpists overseas where it is not possible to send the harp to the factory. It is not recommended that harpists try to have any but the routine jobs of regulation and maintenance done on their instruments except by qualified harp repairmen. Still we will try to provide as much information as possible for those emergencies which must be dealt with when they occur.

No guarantee of the instructions in this book can be implied since both the reader's understanding and skill are outside of our knowledge and control. We do feel, however, that our little book can and will provide valuable assistance as a guide to providing better maintenance and repair for your harp.

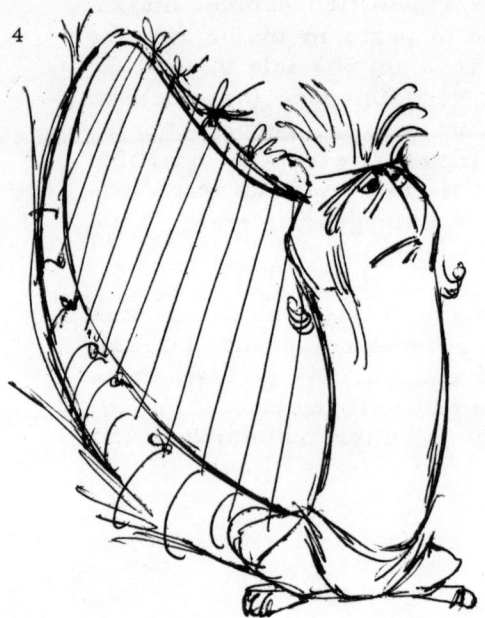

The harp has evolved
from a crude primitive instrument...

... to the mechanical marvel
we play today.

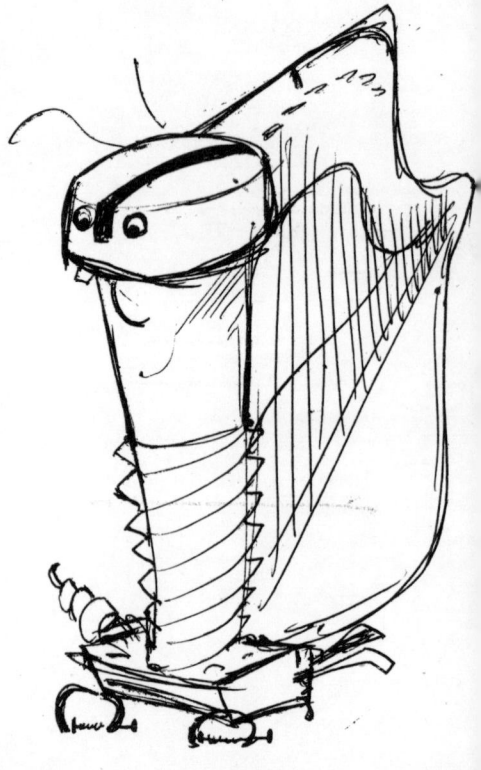

CHAPTER TWO: HISTORY

Probably the first harp was used to shoot arrows much of the time, and in recounting the tale of the hunt the plucked bow-string provided the first background music to an adventure story. Both background music and the harp have come a long way since those days.

Primitive harps resembling the hunter's bow may still be found in use today. Usually six or seven strings have been added, and often some kind of sound board or sound chamber to amplify the sound is attached to the bow, now in the shape of a wide curved "C." This harp is much the same as the harps used by the Egyptians in that they both lack the fore-pillar or column.

The lack of the pillar of the harp makes the frame construction stretching the strings rather unstable, and intonation becomes difficult in the extreme. The problem being that if one string is tightened it pulls the "C" frame more closed, thus loosening all the other strings. The chore of delicately balancing the tensions of the various strings may have been one of the primary reasons why the Egyptian harpist, and harp, are now extinct.

The addition of the column or fore-pillar perhaps sometime in the second millenium B.C. provided a more rigid, although still not completely rigid, frame which could more easily balance the string tensions. From this point the rigid frame was varied to form many kinds of harps, the ancestors of all the string instruments.

THE WANDERING TROUBADOURS

In the middle ages the harp appeared in a recognizable

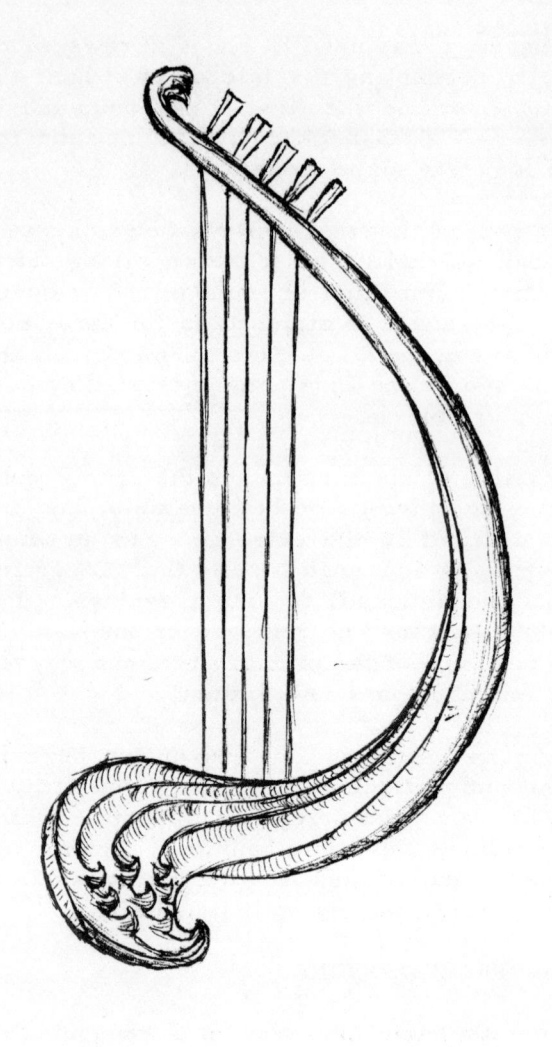

A form of the Egyptian style of harp.

form with a more or less rigid frame and a plurality of strings, providing a scale of some form or other, usually modal, and likely tuned to the particular requirements of the harpist, who often as not accompanied his own ballads and songs. The harp in these times was held in high regard by royalty, and the harpists of the ancient druids held rank just above that of a teacher, and only a little below that of a priest. In Ireland, anciently, slaves and women were forbidden - on pain of death - to touch the harp. As mentioned above, the harp has come a long way.

HOCHBRUCKER'S PEDAL HARP

The chromatic harp with a string for each semi-tone has cropped up from time to time and in various forms and places; however, technique, intonation and other problems known only to its players kept the instrument from assuming a real usefulness. The single action harp was devised about 1720 by Simon Hochbrucker and two or three other clever inventors, all of whom seemed to have worked it out independently and contemporarily.

SEBESTIEN ERARD

Sebestien Erard in Paris about 1810 perfected a double action harp which set the harp on its way into a new era. It is interesting to note that there was, even then, a number of harpists who would have nothing to do with the new type double action harp in spite of the obvious advantages. It has always been difficult, it seems, for harpists to forsake the old in favor of the new; important changes always obtaining only with a new generation; but this type of thinking, so pronounced among older harpists, may be disappearing.

The harp has always had an aura of mystery about it.

GEORGE DURKEE

In about 1877 an American named George Durkee began work on a new type of double action harp for the Lyon & Healy Music Co. It was to be more rugged and easier to adjust, "in order to stand the long journeys, rough handling and climatic problems" common to the United States. He created an excellent harp and his type of action has been the model for all harps designed since his day.

The differences are interesting. They included the possibility of regulating each disc individually, not possible without drastic means on the old Erard. The natural or upper disc was made to remain motionless while the sharp or lower disc completed its movement. The pedal rods were enclosed in brass tubes which gave a much freer action and were not so affected by dampness. A short time later, the extended sounding board was added to the Lyon Healy harp, making the sound board wider at the lower end where the heavier strings needed greater amplification.

Still more recently, in 1958, a new model harp was developed using the principle of flat planes in addition to the sound-board to increase carrying power. The guitar used this principle to drive the lute into obscurity as did the entire viol family with their basically flat backs. In 1956 the troubadour harp was developed, but was not introduced into the harp world until five years later. It almost completes the cycle and takes the harp back to one of its early forms, but with refinements in construction and tone.

The history of the harp is fraught with wonder and magic which our little tracing of its development cannot begin to suggest. Without question, it seems to be unique among musical instruments and we can only agree without further elaboration, "there is something about a harp!"

The harp has five major parts
and about two thousand minor ones.

CHAPTER THREE: HOW THE HARP IS MADE

As Lyon Healy, Inc, has been virtually the only manufacturer of harps since they began in 1889, an exception being the Wurlitzer Company, which produced some very fine instruments until about 1933, we need not apologize for the source of our material being the Lyon Healy harp factory in Chicago. This then will be how harps are made there. The names applied to the various parts will be the names used there; thus, we hope to achieve a certain standardization.

THE HARP IS HANDMADE

The harp is not mass produced; in fact, it is not even produced in assembly line fashion. Harps are made in pairs from start to finish by one master craftsman. Some parts and pieces are roughly pre-formed for him by other craftsmen and the final assembly as well as the carving and gilding are done by specialists of many years experience. These men know and love their chosen craft and their names have been connected with master craftsmanship for many years. Some of the names are: Blaha, Stepeck, Puls, Kolek, Matejka, Heinrick, Zelek, Snegowski, Wagner and Djieman. Harps made since 1959 may have the autograph of the maker inside the body on the under side of the sound-board.

ONE MAN OPERATION

The harp begins very much like a small boat. Four body strips of spruce about four feet long are fitted and glued from the top body block to the bottom body frame, and small spruce ribs are fitted between the body strips. Then two pre-formed shells of four layers of maple each,

Don Juan's Entstehen in Prag.

Und nun zu Mozart's Lied nebst Anhang.

Die folgende Geschichte ist nach Weber's eigenen Worten erzählt:

Mozart composed this theme in Prague for his harpist host to use in improvising fariations. A facsimile of a page in the book "Don Juan" by Freisauff.

glued and curved in a special mold under heat and pressure, are glued to the two sides of the frame structure. Two of these bodies are then given to the master craftsman who trims them, fits in the back panel, the wings, makes the sound-board and glues and screws it to the body. Then he makes the neck, glues on the veneers, drills and reams the tuning-pin holes to a taper so that the tuning-pins will be tight enough to hold the string tension. Then, taking a column that has been carved for him, he fits the neck to it, sands it to a perfectly smooth finish and makes a preliminary assembly with the baseboard and base which he has also made.

Each piece of a harp is made especially for that harp and is not interchangeable with any other. In working with wood and handcrafting it, variations occur due to the nature of the material; thus fittings, adjustments, etc, are constantly necessary in the creation of a harp.

After many such fitting assemblies, all the wooden pieces of the harp match perfectly and are ready to have the lacquer finish sprayed on. This is done by a finishing specialist and expert. Many, that is five or six, coats of highest quality lacquer are sprayed on the harp and each coat is allowed to harden and then is rubbed down before the next coat is applied.

Now the neck is glued and screwed into the column by the craftsman and the pieces are taken to the final assembly room. Here the action is fastened to the neck, the pedal-rod tubes fixed inside the column, the body attached to the base-board, both of which are then attached to the column by one large screw from the base-board to the column. This large screw and a peg from the knee-block to the top of the body mostly keep the column neck and

Ninety-five percent of the harps made since 1889 are still playing.

body properly positioned. They are really held together by the string tension. Now it is beginning to look like a harp. The pedal assembly is fastened to the bottom, the strings are put on and pulled up to pitch. After they have been kept up to pitch for two or three days it is regulated. It has been about three months since the harp was begun.

ELECTRONICALLY REGULATED

The regulation is done with the assistance of a Stroboconn. This is an electronic device which makes it possibile to regulate far more accurately than with the ear alone. Its little whirling dials show each of the twelve semi-tones of the octave with perfect accuracy, and the discs can be made to raise the string pitch by exactly one half-step. The harp is, of course, a tempered instrument.

Now the harp is ready to ship and is fitted into a trunk. The right size blocks are fixed into the trunk to give this particular harp the maximum protection.

Factory production has averaged about seven or eight harps per month. These are distributed only through the Lyon Healy Harp Salons and are shipped all over the United States and the world. Since harps are so well and carefully made, probably ninety-five percent of all the harps Lyon Healy has ever made since 1889 are still in use.

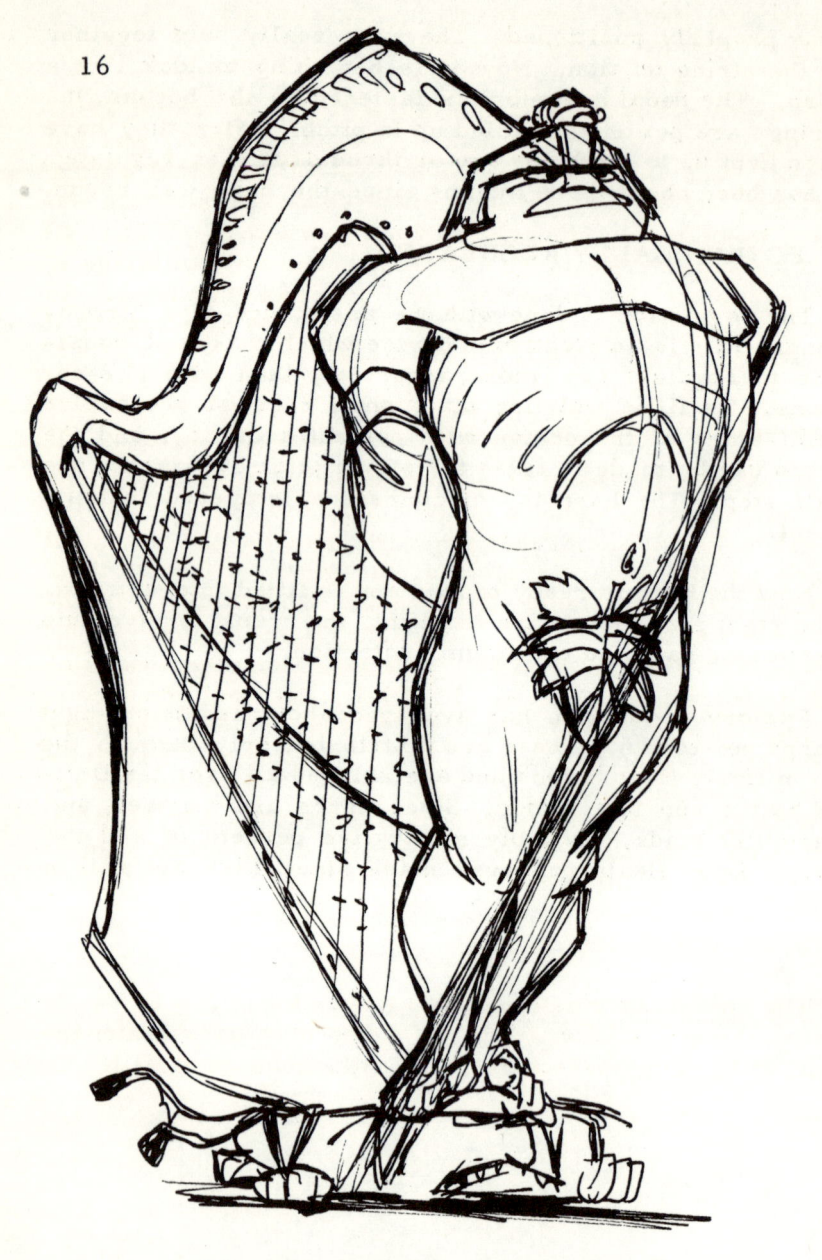

The great harpists of the past
have nearly always been men.

CHAPTER FOUR: HARPISTS, LITERATURE AND TECHNIQUE OF THE PAST

In writing this section our purpose is to try to bring vividly to the attention of today's young harpists, and old ones if such there be, the high level of technical ability that was had by harpists long since dead. In our vain society we belive so strongly in the evolution of all things that we suppose whatever is the present state of things is without doubt the finest and best that has ever been. As far as sheer technical ability on the harp is concerned, it would appear that this is not the case.

REMEMBER THESE NAMES

Music for the harp is a source of many loud and long complaints from some of today's harpists, who decry the great lack of it and at the same time eschew the output of many of the great harpists of the past. A few of their names: Dussek, Mayer, Krumpholtz, Desargus, Parish-Alvars, Albert Zabel, Alphonse Hasselmans, Hans Trnecek, Wilhelm Posse, Marcel Tournier, Gabriel Verdalle, Alfred Holy, F. Dizi, Edmund Schuecker, Francois-Joseph Naderman, Felix Godefroide, Theodore Labarre, Voldemar Loukine, N. Bochsa, Henriette Renie, Ludwig Spohr, and even E. T. A. Hoffman! These are listed neither in order of importance, nor of time, but simply as some of the names that the sincere student of the harp should know.

CHECK THE LIBRARIES

The volume of music put out by even these few is really astonishing. Much of it, to be sure, may have little appeal to our audiences today, but still much of it will. To

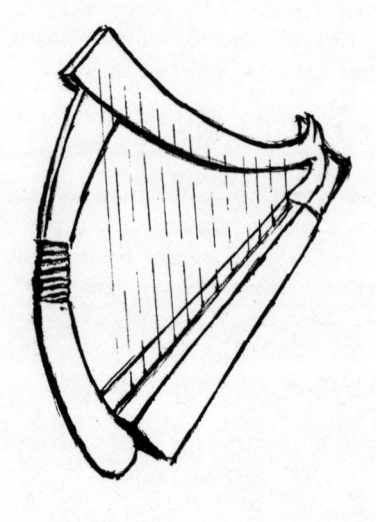

Traditional style of the authentic Irish harp.

ignore it is to rob oneself and one's students of some useful and enjoyable harp music.

DEFENDERS OF THE HARP

The harp was strongly supported by the Irish from the twilight of history at least down through the seventeenth century when Cromwell and his followers in purging the Irish of their organs, etc., also fell upon their harps with such vehemence that they well nigh eliminated that instrument from the land. Beginning in 1600, however, the eclipsing of the harp was more a result of increased popularity of the viol than of national purges; but still the harp retained a great place in the musical culture of Britain and the European nations.

PRIMITIVE HARPS IN USE TODAY

Many harpists who have heard artists from Paraguay and Mexico as well as some of the other Latin American countries perform are usually astonished at the amazing agility these artists have. The limitations of a non-modulating harp are more than compensated by truly brilliant techniques. This may be the germ of the very thing we are investigating. Before the pedal harp, harpists worked for brilliance through finger technique.

FROM THE HEARTH INTO THE ORCHESTRA

The harp was used in an orchestra by Monteverde in his Orfeo, produced in 1607 and heard in band and orchestra at various places through that century. Gluck was also one of the very early users of the orchestral harp. Still, it was not until 1719 that it began to be seriously considered as an orchestral instrument. Handel deserves the gratitude of all harpists for the introduction of the harp into his orchestral scores. His oratorio, "Esther," produced at Canons in 1732 uses the harp most effectively in combination with the arch-lute in accompanying the song, "Breathe Soft, Ye Winds."

HARP COUNTED AS KEYBOARD INSTRUMENT

Alessandro Scarlatti, the father of the prolific composer, Domenico, was known as a harpist during his early years, that is 1673 to 1683, and even a quick examination of some of his compositions, i. e. his Seven Toccatas, shows the marked influence of the harp in his composition. Typical four-finger patterns and other characteristics of early harp music are present. It must be remembered also that the harp generally used for such compositions would be the Italian Doppio Arpa. Such an instrument is noted on the orchestral scores mentioned above. It is a chromatic harp with a string for every semi-tone, and the exact shape and design might vary from maker to maker.

GERMAN HARPIST COMPOSERS
AT THE FRENCH COURT

Leopold Mozart wrote to the wife of Hagenar in Salzburg about life and music in the French court with much distaste for the French composers but great admiration for the person and apartment of the Lady Pompadour. He mentions the leading composers of the Court as being German: "The Germans take the lead. Among them, Schobert, Eckard and Hannauger for clavier, and Hochbrucker and Mayer for harp are very popular." Such an off-hand manner of including harp composers with clavier composers suggests that the two instruments were of nearly equal importance at that time.

THE LOST HAYDN TRIO

Haydn's father is reputed to have been a vocalist and a harper. It is quite well known that Haydn wrote a trio for flute, harp and bass, but the manuscript has never been found. Johann Krumpholz has been called "Haydn's harpist," and indeed he was at Esterhazy for the years from 1773 to 1776. During this period, Haydn produced twelve piano sonatas. Five of them, all published in 1776, differ strongly from the others and are easily played on the harp. They are also very much like the harp music of the period, including Krumpholz's own, so it is highly probable that they were conceived for the harp, or that the harp was to be a ready alternate instrument for them. These may be found in the Peters Edition of the Haydn piano sonatas, Vol. II nos. 12, 13, 14; Vol. III no. 30; Vol. IV no. 36. Look them up and try them for yourself. The chronological numbering is 25, 26, 27, 28 and 29.

THE HAYDN HARP CONCERTO FOR EXAMPLE

Recently, a catalogue listing the "'Premier Concerto pour la Harpe' par M. Joseph Haydn" was called to our attention. The rare music catalogue indicated that the dealer had only the first violin part available from an edition published about 1790 by H. Naderman, Ed., in Paris. Trembling with excitement, we rushed to obtain this single violin part. From this we learned that it was "avec accompagnement de deux violons, alto, basse, deux hautbois et deux cors, ad libitum." Also we learned that it was "arrangé par M. Rague."

The fact that it was listed as "Premier Concerto" pour la Harpe par M. J. Haydn" first and the arranger was listed on the bottom of the title page held our hopes up for further examination. This could mean, we reasoned, that Haydn did indeed write the work for the harp, and that it was expanded or reworked to some degree by the mysterious M. Raguè.

ORIGINAL IN C

The violin part shows that the concerto was originally in C, but the work is now published as the D Major Piano (harpsichord) Concerto op. 21 and has been generally available as such for many years. The original Haydn manuscript of this work has never been found, (one point for the harp) but has been edited from editions published during Haydn's lifetime and more or less revised by him. (Note that "revised" scores two points for the harp.)

An actual examination of the concerto solo part as it is now published has convinced us even further that Haydn not only wrote the work for the harp, but that he was well acquainted with the instrument. Passages that seemed a little awkward to us on the piano lay precisely under the hand on the harp. In the modern publication it has seemed necessary to augment the piano part considerably, extending simple repeated third accompaniments by an added octave, duplication of melodic passages in a lower octave, transposing certain passages an octave higher and otherwise filling out the original rather simple and "harpistic" solo part. Haydn was careful not to go above the E above high C, even to the extent of inverting the theme in the last movement. Perhaps this could indicate the upper limitation of the harp for which he was writing.

GOOD HARP WRITING

The thematic material is characteristic of the harp

writing of the period; in fact the opening theme is an arpeggiated four note chord. A small chromatic passage on the last beat of measure 57 is nicely played on the harp, especially if the passage is put back into the key of C where the pedal changes are divided with one in each foot. The Cadenzas, which in our Peters edition (not in the supplement) are said to have been written by Haydn himself, are strikingly harpistic! In the finale, measure 159 has an upward scale that could not be more effectively played than as a simple scale glissando. "Ah!" our critics will cry, "What of the long chromatic scale in measures 295 and 296 in the last movement?" Well, we retort, what of it? The sustained harmony just before this passage would suggest a simple D major scale or glissando to be even more proper than the indicated chromatic scale which may well have been added in a revision in an effort to capture some of the brilliance of the harp in the same spot.

The above rationalization is at best a theory, since there is no way of proving such a claim; but since we are well aware of the freedom of interchange in all keyboard music of that period, the harpist certainly has as valid a claim to this most charming concerto as any pianist. It is clearly evident that it was performed on the harp during Haydn's lifetime, and perhaps never since. This is all the more regretable. We commend it to all harpists. It can be played in the key of D on our modern harps, and the orchestral parts are easily obtained in this key. The only change that need be made from the Peter's edition is to make the long chromatic scale near the end of the last movement a D major scale covering the range indicated. It will probably be best to stay with the original Haydn and leave out the small notes which have been added by the editor.

We hope the above will also serve as a guide and encouragement to others who may catch a hint of a long lost work for harp and help them to see the important signs to look for.

CONTERTINO FOR HARP AND ORCHESTRA, MENDELSSOHN?

In line with this, we have heard rumors from Mr. N. Zabaleta that reference is made to a Concertino for harp and orchestra by Mendelssohn in a contemporary History of the Harp by Schiringi. Now here is a really worth while piece of research for some ambitious person. Good hunting!

HARP? J. S. BACH?

In the catalogue of J. S. Bach's works, Schmieder shows the E major suite, which elsewhere appears among the violin sonatas, as for "Harp?" A quick examination of it shows that it is neatly divided between the hands, and even the judicious use of harmonics, which were well known long before Bach, would make it a most effective harp solo. It is listed as having been composed in Leipzig in 1737 for the prince of Anahlt Cöthen, a noted amateur instrumentalist enthusiast of the time. (See Schmieder, Verz.1006a. Bach Gesammausgabe BGA-XLII-16)

Most music of the period for keyboard instruments was interchanged readily between the clavier, harpsichord and also the harp. It was also taken for granted that the repeat of any section was to be embellished, ornamented or even freely developed by the performer. In fact, it was the rule for the performer to play almost entirely his own music, composing being an indispensable part of the performing art.

In all ages and in all countries the harp
has been regarded as a celestial instrument.

As often as not, the harp was used in the capacity of a continuo, a part today that is almost entirely relegated to the harpsichord in the mistaken interest of historical accuracy. In many performances of oratorios etc, today, the harp could be used without the extra troubles of obtaining a harpsichord and player, and is preferable, in the light of historical accuracy, to a piano. This noble instrument being far more different from the sound anticipated by the composer than either the harp or the harpsichord.

THE INTERCHANGING HARP

The interchanging of harp and keyboard music was most common even down to the time of Beethoven as is evidenced by his comment in a letter to J. A. Streicher in 1796:

"There is no doubt that as far as the manner of playing it is concerned, the pianoforte is still the least studied and least developed of all instruments: often one thinks that one is merely listening to a harp. And I am delighted, my dear fellow, that you are one of the few who realize and perceive that, providing one can feel the music, one can also make the pianoforte sing. I hope that the time will come when the harp and the pianoforte will be treated as entirely different instruments."

Here we see that it is not just the interplaying of their music that Beethoven is protesting, but that the very concept of composing and performing for the two were too similar!

THE HARP-LIKE PIANO

The piano sound of the period was much more like a

harp than the grand piano of today. It had only a single string per note, and the hammer was covered with leather rather than felt. This produced a tone with little body and the hammer blow sounded more like a plucked string, a mellow harpsichord sound, or even more like a harp sound. An instrument similar to this constructed in our day is called the "Mozart Piano." Appropriate works played on it have even greater charm than on our modern piano. The line of each part is followed with greater ease due to the nature of the tone. The smaller sound, which is more pointed, leads toward greater attention put to the lines and figurations, rather than bombarding the listener with a compelling fortissimo. All things that harpists have had to be aware of for years.

DID MOZART DISLIKE THE HARP?

Mozart's alleged dislike of the harp may actually have been a mis-quote recorded by one of his ex-students, Dr. Joseph Frank. This chance remark may have obscured some of the charm not only of the Mozart Flute and Harp Concerto, but every other usage of these instruments by this master. Mozart was actually quite enthusiastic about the harpistic ability of the daughter of the Duc de Guines. In a letter to his father in 1778, he says of his student: She . . . "plays the flute extremely well, and the harp 'magnifique.'"

MOZART'S OTHER COMPOSITIONS FOR THE HARP

It has always been difficult to believe that with the widespread use of the harp, as judged from engravings of the period and the record of the French Court, that Mozart did not write more for the instrument, especially since he had a harpist for a student. We can see from the tradition of the period, that harpists may have been welcome to what pieces of his keyboard music they were able to play, but it would seem likely that this genius who could turn out any music on demand would have written some things specifically for the harp.

As a result of the research for this book, two themes have come to light written for the further improvisation of harpists of the day, and also we have found, thanks to Artiss de Volt, a complete "Air and Variations with Rondo Pastoral" written expressly for the harp by W. A. Mozart. The original copy of this is even fingered in the old manner by John Thomas using x for the thumb and 1, 2, & 3 for the 2nd, 3rd and 4th fingers. This is now available with the fingering revised by the author.

NOT SO DIFFICULT

Mozart's Flute and Harp Concerto, for all the trouble it gives harpists today, was not one of the more difficult works for the instrument when it was written. In 1787, when Mozart was in Prague for the premier of Don Giovani, he stayed at an inn where his host was an excellent amateur harpist. For his host's pleasure, as the man delighted in making up variations on a theme, Mozart composed a theme on the spot (Köchel anhang 207a). Since the harpist did not read music, it was given orally, and then later that night written down for posterity. It might be noted here, that the author has written a set of variations on this theme of Mozart.

PRODIGIOUS TECHNIQUE

Examining the music of the period, which was to be played on the harp, or on either the harp or keyboard, we must conclude that there existed a prodigious technique among the players of the time. Judging from the work of harpists from Krumpholtz through Bochsa, the technique of the instrument had reached astonishing heights, and even with their single action harps, chromatic passages were actually taken as a matter of course!

The author must publically apologize for a rather harsh opinion which he held for some time for such harpists as Naderman and Madam Krumpholtz (not Johann), who held on to the single action harp long after the double action was available. It is really astonishing what can be played on a single action harp, and for the music of this period, there is little advantage to be gained with a double action. It was only after a new kind of harp music developed that the single action became really obsolete.

WELSH CHROMATIC HARP

We have learned only recently that the chromatic, double strung harp was in much wider use than has been thought before, and it was only with reluctance that some of the harpists, such as the Welsh harper, Edward Jones, admitted the superior capabilities of the "German Harp" as they called the new pedal action instrument! Surviving works of the period suggest what agility these artists had: single handed trills and tremolos, scale work equal to the pianists of the day, including what we lament as the "five-finger-passage," arpeggios in one and both hands and ornamentation that is dazzling.

PARISH-ALVARS

With this background, then, it is not so surprising when we learn of the phenomonon that was E. Parish-Alvars.

He was the harpist who fascinated Berlioz, charmed Schumann and Mendelssohn and has had a pronounced effect on both orchestration and piano technique since his time. It seems astonishing that perhaps the piano has borrowed devices from the harp that we now ignore because they are too pianistic. The famous Talberg three hand effect, playing the melody between the two thumbs of both hands, with figuration surrounding it, was original with Parish-Alvars from whom Talber learned it!

PIANISTIC PASSAGES?

Theodore Labarre, who was professor at the Paris Conservatoire from 1867 until he died in 1870, produced what has been called the finest method for the harp. But in spite of this and his wonderful achievements as a harpist composer and performer, his music was criticized by Hasselmans as being unsuitable for the harp since it contained many "pianistic passages"! Is the wonderful technique for the harp beginning to be lost at this point?

LISZT AND THE HARP

Parish-Alvars was not the only harpist to attract the attention of Franz Liszt. Here is a quotation from a letter written by Liszt in 1884 to Wilhelm Posse:

> Dear fellow artist and friend,
> It is always a real joy to marvel at your brilliant, glittering and thoroughly musical capabilities. I would particularly thank you for your kind readiness to play harp solos at the next Tonkunstler (Music Society) meeting at Weimar...

If you would allow me, I would like to recommend that you play on this occasion either Parish-Alvars' Oberon transcription or the E Major Etude by Chopin and the third of my Liebestraume so splendidly transcribed by yourself. Perhaps you could also find room for the Angelus.

F. Liszt

TRANSCRIPTIONS

Like most of the work of Parish-Alvars, the Oberon transcription is now extinct, but imagine playing the E Major Etude of Chopin on the harp with the chromaticism in the middle section! Or even the third Liebestraume and the Angelus by Liszt. The author has the three Liebestraume transcribed by Posse and his variations on the well known "Carnival of Venice." The former lose nothing in being played on the harp, and the latter is the best set of variations we've ever heard on the theme. Nowadays it is quite out of fashion to play "airs and variations" but we fear that this is a tragic loss because of our snobbery. They are wonderful fun. As far as technique is concerned, these pieces and transcriptions are far more demanding on the capabilities of the harpist than almost all of the solo harp music heard in our recitals today.

What has happened to the harp technique of today? Has it been gradually lost so that now any works of a classical style requiring "finger-work" are regarded as "pianistic," and therefore unsuitable for the harp? Did the advent of the double action harp and with it the glissando arpeggio weaken the finger technique of the harpist?

HENRIETTE RENIE

Certainly the great tradition of fearless technique and

the demand of such in compositions and transcriptions is evidenced in the works of Mme. H. Renie. Twelve books of her transcriptions of the classics are available and all are well and tastefully done. Much of such classic literature needs nothing more than the pedalling added, but judicious fingering indications from a person of great experience are certainly worth while. Besides this particular series, Renie has made transcriptions of major works of Chopin, Liszt, Debussy, Bach and many other excellent composers. Many of her own compositions rank among the finest works for harp. Try her "Danse des Lutins"; it makes a good measuring stick for your own technique.

HARPISTS OF THE PRESENT

If future historians wonder at the omission of a name from this volume, they will have to forgive us because it is a risky business to name names among one's contemporaries. Giants sometimes emerge unexpectedly, and the great may only seem so because they are near.

Perhaps it would be better for future generations to wonder why a name is not in our book than to wonder why it is.

Most large orchestras employ
both a first and a second harp.

CHAPTER FIVE: THE ORCHESTRAL HARPIST

The real victim of the loss in brilliant harp technique will be primarily the orchestral harpist. It is now an all too common practice for harpists to begin thinking of ways to simplify or rewrite a part before they have even tried to conform with the composer's indications. This is actually as morally wrong as stealing. The harpist is hired to play a certain part. The composer has written it and prescribed what should be played. The other instruments of the orchestra play their parts, and no less should be expected of the harpist. Composers are not as ignorant of the harp, or at least as devoid of common sense, as they are often suspected of being. If you do want to change something a composer has written, make sure that it is not because of your own inadequacies rather than the composer's ignorance of the harp.

EVER PRACTICE WITH YOUR EYES CLOSED?

Many orchestral harpists have difficulty because they have never learned, that is practiced, playing the harp without looking at it. Indeed some will maintain that it is not possible, though a quick glance at history, and the many excellent blind harpers proves that such is not the case. It may be that harpists begin to concentrate on learning pieces for their repertoire before they have gained all their technique, and their eyes become tied to the strings. Others perhaps become too conscious of looking pretty at all times rather than playing really well. Even as little as fifteen minutes spent sight-reading each day will prove to the harpists that they can learn to sight-read and will also greatly free their eyes for the conductor.

A HARPIST IS TRAPPED

In general, it seems that the poor harpist is rather trapped by circumstance. The urgent need for performers on the harp means that the neophite harpist will probably be pressed into service with some orchestra as soon as he has learned how to hold his hands, the harp, and the place in the music. Then, time, or the lack of it, will begin to crystallize him at that level of technique simply because he must use practice time to learn orchestral parts. If he could spend more time improving his playing and technique, most of the parts could be almost sight-read, rather than almost played-from-memory.

We also find in a few cases harpists who have won an orchestral chair think they have arrived, and that there is no higher level to which they can aspire, or else they are perfectly happy just playing as they do and where they do. More's the pity!

As soon as a performer on any instrument begins to spend more time learning literature or repertoire than they do in learning technique, that is, scales, arpeggios and etudes, they will stop at that level, and only with great effort and difficulty improve from then on.

HARP IN THE STANDARD ORCHESTRAL REPERTOIRE

There is a great deal of music that has become pretty standard fare in this country, though it does vary somewhat from nation to nation, so if young harpists would play a good audition and save themselves a lot of work during the seasons ahead, they should know and even own their own parts to at least the following orchestral compositions:

Berlioz,	Fantastic Symphony
Bizet,	L'Alesienne Suites I & II
	Carmen Suite
Borodin,	Polovetzian Dances
Brahms,	German Requiem
Bruch,	Scotch Fantasy
Chabrier,	Espana
Debussy,	Afternoon of a Faun
	Iberia
	La Mer
	Nocturnes
Dvorak,	Carnival Overture
Faure,	Requiem
	Pelleas et Melisande Suite
Franck,	Symphony in D Minor
Liszt,	Les Preludes
Ravel,	Daphnis et Chloe
	La Valse
	Mother Goose Suite
	Tzigane
Rimsky-Korsakov,	Capriccio Espagnol
	Russian Easter Overture
	Scheherazade
Sibelius,	Pohjola's Daughter
	The Swan of Tuonela
Smetana,	The Moldau
Strauss, R.,	Death and Transfiguration
	Don Juan
	Heldenleben
Stravinsky	Firebird Suite
Tschaikowsky	Nutcracker Suite
	Romeo and Juliet Overture
	Sleeping Beauty Suite
	Swan Lake Suite

Wagner,   Tristan and Isolde, Orchestral Suite
                    Magic Fire Music from Die Walküre
                    Prelude to Die Meistersinger
Weber   Invitation to the Dance

Most of these harp parts can easily be obtained from Lyon Healy. Not all of them are terribly difficult, although some are extremely so. Serious orchestral harpists should make sure that they are familiar with all the above list. No doubt there are many other important pieces which should have been included. Almost no contemporary compositions have been listed since few of them are played regularly enough to be called part of the standard repertoire.

TUNING WITH TROMBONES AND TYMPANI

Orchestral harpists will probably never get the absolute silence they would like to have, unless they are at the hall an hour or so early, and even then the piano tuner will most likely be there. A harp will go out of tune within an hour anyway, so you had better work out a system of tuning under duress. A couple of tricks may help. Put your ear against the knee-block, or on the top of the neck and you can hear the harp very well in spite of great noise; but beware of two problems: don't throw your back out of joint from the physical contortions necessary to tune the bass strings and keep your ear on the harp; secondly, the tone is a little distorted when listening against the harp this way, so your tuning may not be as accurate until you get used to it. Keep trying, it will work out, and then you can happily ignore all kinds of racket.

Make friends with the men who
move and care for your harp.

TUNE A LITTLE SHARP

Make friends with the oboe player, if he still gives the pitch, and get to know where he will put it. Make your pitch at least a couple of beats sharp. A sharp harp sounds better than a flat one, and the string section will soon be above the oboe's pitch anyway. If you tune in naturals the minor regulation problems will not be as bad in the various key changes. Even if your harp is perfectly regulated, it is a good idea to check the intonation of the solo passages in the program and make any necessary adjustments in your tuning.

THE STAGE HANDS ARE YOUR BEST FRIENDS

A clever harpist will quickly recognize that they are pretty much at the mercy of the men who move the harp. Make them your friends. Not only will they take better care in moving your instrument, but very often they are on very casual terms with the conductor and an unkind word about an inconsiderate harpist may make a difference in the management's attitude toward you. Also, don't forget that the truckers or others who move your harp should be your buddies, too.

CRYING IN THE ORCHESTRAL WILDERNESS

The harp is not a loud instrument and may seem to be easily covered by the rest of the orchestra. Actually this may be the composer's intention. The harp can add a pedal effect to the orchestra, not unlike the sustaining pedal of the piano, and in this capacity adds greatly to the color of the ensemble almost without being heard. Coupled with the brass section, the harp seems to be covered almost to the point of its being no use playing; but hear Die Meistersinger Overture by Wagner and notice the excellent bell like quality imparted to the loud trumpets, trombones and tuba by our poor, weak and almost inaudible harp. Not so unimportant after all, is it?

Perhaps we, as harpists, spend so much of our time as soloists that we think because our part in the orchestra is not always a solo it is not important or even heard. Actually, you are part of the orchestral team, and though very often you may be a soloist, you are not always the prima donna.

DON'T CHEAT YOURSELF

After the question of too loud, comes the complaint too fast. This again is a lack of ability on the part of the harpist. If you can play a passage slowly, but not as fast as the composer and conductor may require it, you simply can't play the passage. Go back and practice some more. In brief take pride in not cheating. There is great satisfaction in working out and playing an impossible passage.

Even tho' they may seem to have a small tone, some harps have great carrying power.

CHAPTER SIX: ON THE QUALITY OF HARP MUSIC

SNOBBERY AND IGNORANCE

It is with disappointment not unmixed with some slight pity that one reads statements of prominent harpists to the effect that great harp virtuosi of the past had no real talent for composition and that the mere studying and performance of their works is tantamount to musical stupidity. This bespeaks musical snobbery and ignorance of the worst possible order, particularly when it must be realized that such a person has probably never heard more than the slightest fraction of the musical product of such composers, much less played or studied any of it! They only repeat parrot-like what they have been told and never examine the evidence for themselves.

NARROW MINDS AND REPERTOIRES

This may just point out a prevalent problem. Each teacher, and the author is also guilty, has a tendency to use primarily his own compositions, some going even so far as to use nothing that they have not written or transcribed. All other compositions are dismissed as having been written by unimportant composers who either had no talent for musical composition or did not know how to write for the harp. Merely being aware of this problem vividly points up the solution. Don't maintain a narrow mind or repertoire. Do examine and re-examine available material. You may change an opinion with time and experience.

GREAT MUSIC?

Only a small portion of any gross musical output can be

called great, whether it is music written in the nineteenth century or the twentieth, or even the twelfth. If it has survived for more than three generations and is still played and loved, the chances are excellent, according to Ernst Toch, that it is great music. Thus we can conclude that music remaining to us from these early harp composers, if it has been well known since its composition and is still loved and played, may even be great music. Great music does not have to be the Ninth Symphony of Beethoven. It must only fill a need and do it well.

JOIN THE HUNT

We do have a few such pieces from the early harpists and one of the first that comes to mind is "La Source" by Zabel. This piece has been sure-fire with audiences for at least seventy five years. How many others could be lying hidden away because they seem difficult with our present type of technique or simply because the economy of a publisher has made them out of print?

We recently found two waltzes by Wm. Posse that are as charming for the harp as the Chopin waltzes are for piano. A "Novelette" by Trnecek, recently come by, certainly rivals those of Schumann. A "Furiante" by the same composer is one of the most brilliant pieces we know of for the harp, and there are precious few of such.

Join the hunt. Check the music department of every library to which you may have access. Many fine collections of music have been bequeathed to some great institution only to lie in boxes or on shelves and molder away. Most libraries have a copying service or can arrange for photostates or microfilming. Get copies of likely looking pieces and share them with your friends and the Harp Society. They may be developing a library of such rare harp music that maybe one day a publisher will arise to his obligation and make it generally abailable. Remember that even J. S. Bach bad to be rediscovered and brought to the attention of the music world by Felix Mendelssohn!

PROGRAM NEW OR DIFFERENT WORKS

We have mentioned in this volume a number of pieces of harp music almost never played. The five likely sonatas of Haydn are charming on the harp and would grace any program. Look them up and see for yourself. Check out the other harp composers we've mentioned. Try Alessandro Scarlatti. Whether his compositions now available were written for the harp or key-board, they show great harp characteristics such as four finger patterns and other identifying mannerisms that brand him as a harpist.

SONGS WITHOUT WORDS

It is recorded in the history of the Rothschild family that one of their daughters was sent to study the harp with of all people, Rossini and Mendelssohn! We have long been intrigued by the decidedly harpistic style of Mendelssohn's "Songs Without Words" and wondered if he did not actually have the harp well in mind when he conceived most of them. Since it is also recorded that Parish-Alvars, whose span of life incidentally coincides almost exactly with Mendelssohn's, had met the composer, perhaps more of these excellent pieces than "The Poet's Harp" were inspired by our cherished instrument. It would be well worth a little more looking into. Meanwhile, here we have forty-eight lovely compositions which can legitimately be used in harp recitals!

A WORD ABOUT PROGRAMMING

Traditional programming requires that the performer begin with a work from the baroque or classic period and then proceed more or less chronologically through to the end. This is not a bad idea and is quite safe. It need not be a hard and fast rule however, but watch out that numbers early in the program do not over-shadow what follows. The concept to keep in mind might be that what follows must in a way "top" what preceeded, not necessarily in brilliance but perhaps in harmonic variation or difference in style. If a composition on the program does not really top what came before, it should at least offer some contrast. One more danger to watch out for: Don't allow the program to break up into a hodge-podge of little pieces. Organize the short pieces into logical groups of about three or four as if they were the movements of a sonata or suite. The groups can be all of the same composer or of music of similar style, or pieces with some other good reason why they should be played together. Try to program two or three large works, such as a suite or a sonata which can serve to fill a group by itself. They will help to lend solidarity to the program. Also keep in mind your own best abilities in your choice of selections. It is a good idea to end with something rather brilliant with a rousing finale that will get the audience to respond. Many listeners don't decide how well they liked a concert until they hear their applause. It is just good salesmanship to persuade them that they thought you were great.

PROGRAM YOUR OWN WORKS, IF THEY ARE GOOD

Try writing music yourself, or encourage your composer friends to write for you and above all, play their compositions. Maybe they won't all be good, but greater quantity will almost certainly increase that small percentage of great quality.

CHAPTER SEVEN: GLISSANDOS AND HARMONICS

GIVE ME A WHACHAMACALLIT!

The question of standardization on the harp extends not only just to the names of the parts, but also to the music and notation as well. One of the intentions of the American Harp Society is to make certain accepted names for peculularly harpistic effects standard; i. e., a series of notes, a scale tuned to any desired pedal combination and played by sliding the thumb or finger up or down the harp, is called a glissando. It has at various times been given other names such as sdrucciolando, or more recently, flux. But even those who call it a flux will explain almost in the same breath that "flux" means glissando. Composers and arrangers all know this effect and call it by the name "glissando."

HARMONICS ARE WRITTEN WHERE THEY ARE PLAYED

Harmonics are indicated by a small circle above the note, as are harmonics on the violin and other string instruments. Like the other string instruments, harmonics should be written for the convenience of the player, or where they are to be played, and sounding one octave higher. This has been standard for many years, the only exception being the later works of Salzedo, in which he wrote harmonics where they sound, apparently for the convenience of any pianist who might play the piece. Lack of conformity with the great majority on this point has only resulted in some confusion, and the evidence of the great majority of harp music should be followed.

OTHER SPECIAL HARP NOTATION

The sign to dampen the vibrating strings is the ⊕ or coda sign. It may be extended by a dotted line to indicate a series of etouffe or staccato notes. Attached to a small note by a long stem it may indicate individual dampenings.

P.d.l.t. means to play near the soundboard, and here also an extended line may indicate to play a whole phrase in this manner. P.d.l.t. segue may be used to indicate that the performer is to continue playing near the sound board until further notice.

Instructions to play with the finger nail, in glissando or otherwise, may be indicated by a crescent ‿ extended by a line for as far as the effect is desired.

Do not expect good practice habits from a student, unless you have taught them good practice procedure.

CHAPTER EIGHT: ON TEACHERS AND TEACHING

A good student of the harp will quickly realize that a good teacher is not necessarily a great performer, and that a person may be one and not the other. As in all instruments, teaching harp may be a full time occupation, and the necessary time to study and practice may no longer be available. It may also be that a person can have an excellent talent for teaching, for understanding the scope of a problem and the way to impart its solution to another person, without being able to demonstrate it himself in a perfected state. Just as another person will be a superb harpist and not have the foggiest notion how to tell another person the way to play a single note.

The scarcity of real teachers of the instrument today puts every harpist, whether they are ten years old or ninety, in the position that they will probably be asked to give some lessons. If you find yourself in this position, do not think that being asked alone, qualifies you as a teacher, or that you should not give what help you can, but honestly and intelligently try to find out what will be the best way of approaching the job. A good book on piano teaching, for example, "On Teaching the Piano" by Hetty Bolton, will provide you with a more systematic approach and many helpful suggestions. Teaching is a different art than harp playing or piano playing. You may know one very well and be helpless because of your ignorance in the other.

GUIDEPOSTS IN TEACHING

It has been said by some that there is no teaching; there is only learning. It is a process of absorbing information and learning skills on the part of the student, and the teacher can only place before him the cumulative experience of the past with the fond hope that it will ease or speed up the process.

STAY ORGANIZED

Present this past experience, yours and others, to your student in an efficient and organized manner. Proceed step by step, each reinforcing what has already been learned and preparing for what is next to come. Keep a goal in your mind and also in the student's mind. Let each step be small enough that the student can recognize progress, but not so slow as to let him become bored nor to neglect his fullest potential.

PRACTICE

Do not expect good practice from a student unless you have taught him good practice procedure. Practice a passage four times slowly for every one time fast. Practice whole pieces this same way, four slow, once fast. Enjoy playing it through without a single mistake. Cultivate perfection. Make exercises of particularly difficult passages and let them become part of your daily warm up. Work on scales in all major and minor keys and arpeggios the same. The Hanon daily studies mentioned elsewhere in this book are superb for building a really excellent technique.

A young student will usually respond better to instructions to practice a passage or piece a certain number of times rather that for a specified period of time. He can waste the time away, but if he must play "Tantum Ergo" twenty five times before he can go out and play, his mind and enthusiasm will stay more alert and it will be done.

Build a desire for perfection and for the highest goals. Help the student to see the beauty in every note so much that he will not want to slight any.

WORK THAT WHICH IS DIFFICULT

When you find a particular type of thing that is difficult for your pupil, rejoice! Here you have a concrete problem you can solve. Accurate definition of a problem is at least half of the solution. Why is it difficult? How is it difficult? How must the hand and fingers move? The feet? Do it in slow motion, not just slowly, but in slow motion. Try to put into language the solution to the problem. It will help to crystallize your thinking on it. Do not expect the exact same answer to two different problems even when they appear to be identical. Keep an open mind.

LEARN YOUR STUDENT

Get to know the pupil. How do they think? What problems do they have? Physical? Emotional? Know their potential and expect, no, insist on, no less than their highest. The best teachers on every instrument have always been those who were the hardest, who were the most demanding and would settle for no less than perfection.

This is a difficult way to teach. How much easier it is to let the student get by with just a little less, since both teacher and student weary of a piece and would like to move on. An answer to this may be in using etudes that are part of a permanent practice plan, such as Hanon exercises or Bochsa or Schmidt etudes that are to be played every day. They then become part of an almost hypnotic routine that dilutes the boredom and still the benefits continue.

LEARN TO LISTEN

If you are being paid for your time, give full measure. Listen, don't day dream or otherwise let your mind wander. Learn what to listen for. Experience more than anything else will teach this. Don't interrupt so often that you prevent the mind of the student from even getting started on the track. Watch your own attitude toward the pupil and check to make sure what prompts your various criticisms. Leave room for the opinions of others. Still, a student should be willing to learn what you have to teach and learn it in your way, or he is wasting his time and money. After he can conform exactly with your requirements, then he may be more in a position to make a choice between your way and his or any other. Never lose your temper. The teacher in a fit of anger does nothing but frighten or disgust the pupil and may also provoke him to anger. No learning can take place when a person is enraged.

CULTIVATE SELF RELIANCE IN A PUPIL

A student who must go on taking lessons for the rest of his life is a pitiful thing indeed. Refresher courses and coaching are excellent and necessary even for the advanced artist, since it is almost impossible for the performer to know how he really sounds, but for a student to be so helpless that he must run to the teacher for every pedalling of a piece or go back to the "master" for the musical interpretation of every new work means he is not a complete musician. After a period of time, a student should be able to begin making decisions and guiding himself somewhat. This should be cultivated by the teacher's asking the pupil how he might finger this or pedal that. They must be able to stand alone some day, or they are of little use to the harp and no credit to the teacher.

BE POSITIVE

Some teachers get the idea that if they tell a student how difficult something is, it will inspire them to work harder to overcome the difficulty. This is psychologically incorrect. It is more conducive to better learning for the student to believe that something is not too difficult. Suggest always the positive aspects in teaching, not always how hard it is or always what is wrong. Mention two things that are good or right for every one that you tell them is wrong. We will admit, however, that this last rule may be difficult to follow with some students.

INSPIRE AND DEVELOP ENTHUSIASM IN YOUR STUDENTS

Without doubt, the most important thing that any teacher must do is to keep up a level of enthusiasm in their students. No amount of success in the other areas will amount to much if the teacher cannot do this. Enthusiasm is what will move the pupil to action. Let the lessons be stimulating. Your method of stimulation may be whatever comes easiest and most natural to you. It may be some kind of pressure for one student or relaxation for another. It may be potential reward or even veiled retribution. But it must keep the student coming back for the next lesson, and induce a certain amount of reflection and practice in between. If you don't enjoy teaching, the student will probably not enjoy learning. Try to find for yourself reasons why you like what you are doing. Use common sense and modern psychology on yourself as well as your student.

MATERIAL

Good teaching will of course require good teaching material. A list of the most commonly used harp methods and studies will be found in the following section.

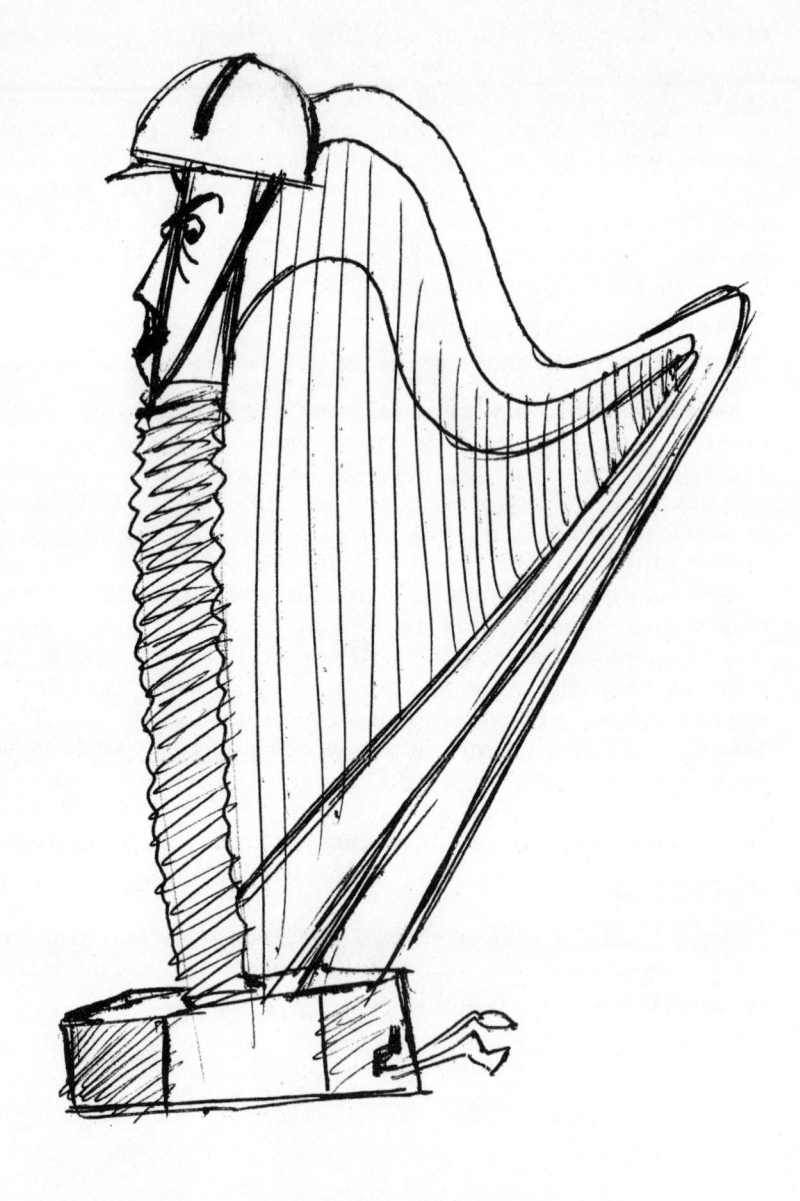

The harp is a demanding instrument.

CHAPTER NINE: FOUNDATION TO EXCELLENT TECHNIQUE

We believe that the foundation of the technique of the great harp virtuosi of the past was founded on some very definite ideas. They had not so many preconceived notions about the limitations of the harp and so lacked the fear of trying something new. They approached passage work and pedal work with the easy optimism of a person who does not know that what he is doing is impossible. They succeeded. Go and do likewise. Do not take for granted that something cannot be played. Try it first.

These great harpists worked for years on technique. Tradition called for a seven year apprenticeship in minstrelsy. They were not expected nor allowed to start building a repertoire before they had built up a good facility on the harp. Etudes were the main fare for the student, and should be even today. We will take the liberty of listing those that are the most used and in our opinion most beneficial.

Bochsa, Op. 318, Quarante Etudes Faciles, Vols. I & II
  Op. 62, Vingt Cinq Exercises Etudes
  Op. 34, Cinquante Etudes, Vols. I & II
  These etudes are the back-bone of the harp study material.

Bochsa-Oberthur, Universal Method for Harp
  As good as any method currently available. Includes Bochsa Op. 318, 40 Easy Studies, which are pleasant and beneficial.

Grossi, Metodo per Arpa
  In Italian only. Has 65 little progressive studies by

Pozzoli. A good method, but does not go as far as the Bochsa-Oberthur.

Hanon, Daily Exercises, edited and fingered by S. O. Pratt, Vols. I, II & III
Simple exercises for strength, agility and evenness; scales and arpeggios in all major and minor keys, chromatic scales, repeated notes, scales in thirds and sixths, broken octaves and arpeggios, trills, tremolos. Indispensable for virtuosity.

Lariviere, ed. Hasselmans-Martenot, Exercises et Etudes pour la Harpe
Seventy-Seven short technical exercises and three etudes of medium difficulty.

Naderman, ed. Hasselmans-Martenot, Sept Sonates Progressive pout la Harpe.
Seven etude sonatinas ranging from medium to medium difficult.

Pozzoli, Studi di Media Difficolta per Arpa
Thirty excellent and interesting studies, more or less progressive.

Renie, Methode complete de la Harpe. Vols. I & II
French only. Very good and most complete. Expensive, must be ordered specially.

Salzedo, Method for the Harp
In English and French, generally not as complete as the other methods listed, lacking much of the elementary material going quickly into medium material. Includes fifteen preludes as etudes, contains the famous Chanson dans la Nuit.

Salzedo, Modern Study of the Harp
  Six excellent etudes covering the range of Salzedo's style. Each develops a special problem. Some suitable for concert use. Section on special effects for the harp.

Schmidt, Six Etudes pour Harpe, Revues par P. Jamet
  Excellent studies, at least four worthy of public performance.

Zabel, Methode fur Harfe, Vols. I, II & III
  Uses the Bochsa Op. 318. Rather wordy in three languages; French, German and English. Much basic exercise material. Some advanced etudes by Zabel.

Posse, Eight Great Concert-Studies for harp
  Extremely difficult, but excellent studies. Some suitable for concert performance. Available separately.

UNUSUAL PROGRAM MATERIAL

Concert pieces that are mostly unusual and not often heard on harp recitals are listed below. We have arbitrarily graded them from easy - 1 to extremely difficult - 7.

Bach, J. S.	Suite in E for Harp -6-
Brahms	Intermezzo in B Flat Minor -6-
Debussy	Jardins sous la Pluie -5-
	Nocturne -5-
	Dr. Gradus ad Parnassum -6-
Cassela, Alfredo	Sonata per Arpa -5-
Grandjany	Children's Hour -6-
Handel-Beon	Passacaille -4-
Ibert	Reflet dans l'Eau -3-
Migot	Sonate Luthee -7-

Mortari	Sonatina Prodigie -6-
Mozart	Air with Variations and Rondo Pastoral -5-
Perilhou-Grandjany	Chanson de Guillot-Martin -4-
Prokofieff	Vision Fugitive no. 5
Purcell-Thomson	Ground in F -2-
Pratt	Variations on Mozart's theme for Harp -6-
	Preludes (5) -5-
	Castilliene Suite -6-
Maghini	Suite Breve, per Arpa, 2nd Suite -5-
Renie	Danse des Lutins
Respighi-Grandjany	Siciliana -6-
Rota	Sarabande e Toccata -5-
Salzedo	Variations on a Theme in Ancient Style -6-
Tournier	Sonatine Op. 30 no. 1 -6-

The above list is presented primarily to bring to harpists' attention some worthwhile harp music, original and transcribed, that is not heard on every recital. There are many more than these, particularly in old compositions that are not readily available and must be photostated.

Recent combined harp festivals have had as many as seventy-two participants.

CHAPTER TEN: FOR COMPOSERS

Writing for the harp seems to terrify some composers while others take to it naturally. Some have a concept of how a harp works and others must labor over it. Actually writing for the harp need not be too difficult. Keep in mind that the harpist will only use four fingers on each hand, and that the hand spacing is upside down from the treble hand of the piano; that is, the wide space between the thumb and first finger will be on top in both hands, so space chords and figurations accordingly. The strings are tuned diatonically in the key of C, and each string may be raised or lowered one half step by means of its pedal. The pedals can be moved very fast, so that coordination of the finger and foot often becomes the problem.

There is very little that a harp cannot play. Debussy wrote his "Sacred and Profane Dances" for the chromatic harp, but they were promptly played on the pedal harp. A fast chromatic scale will never be a grace on the harp, but chromatic changes that can alternate between the two feet are not overly difficult.

The pedals of the harp are arranged thus: D C B // E F G A, looking at the back of the harp. The left foot takes the D C B and the right foot the E F G A. The pedals can be moved two at a time, one with each foot; but many such changes, as on every beat, will keep the harpist off balance and hence are difficult. Pedals may be changed while playing without causing any interruption. They can be changed during a glissando or any other time even though the string is still sounding.

There are three positions for each pedal. The upper is for flat, the middle is natural, and the lower, sharp. A pedal can be moved very rapidly from flat to natural or natural to sharp or the reverse of these. There will be only slightly more difficulty in moving a pedal from flat all the way to sharp or vice versa. Two adjacent pedals on one side or the other may be moved with one foot if they are both moved from the same position, say flat, to the same position, natural. Such an operation is a little risky, but is a little easier for men than for women.

Composers will be wise to mark in their pedal changes for the harpist. It will let them make sure that what they are writing is playable, and also demonstrate to the harpist that the writer does know the harp well enough to write for it. Scales and arpeggios in both hands at the same time are not popular nowadays, and are admittedly difficult, but can be learned if it is important to the composition. Most other kinds of passage-work can be worked out on the harp. Wagner parts are famous among harpists as being hard, but they get learned and played in spite of the complaints.

Examining the harp parts listed in the section on the Orchestral Harpist in this book will give examples of typical harp writing. Further examination of the music written by the harpists listed in this book will give examples of how a harp can be used most effectively.

The harp will never be very loud, and if you write the orchestration with the harp part covered, that is just what you will get. The bass viol with its rich upper partials is especially likely to cover the harp, some times absorbing it even more than the brass section. For judicious use of the harp in really economical scoring, check the scores of Mahler. Every note is effective, though he wrote only a few.

There are better books than ours to outline the orchestrating of the harp; our hope is to outline the pitfalls in the actual harp writing. Reviewing the sections of this book dealing with the harpists and literature of the past will help to arm the potential harp composer for his task, if he will also look up some of the music written for the instrument.

Do not be afraid of the harp. If you can find a mental way to play it, using only the diatonic scale altered by the seven pedals, and with only four fingers on each hand, it can most likely be played. Do check things over with a reliable harpist, but do not be afraid to make them tax themselves. They have been used to easy parts perhaps, and may try to keep things simple enough to be sight-read.

Today the harp world tends to be dominated by women.

CHAPTER ELEVEN: TO MUSIC CRITICS

The music critic is apt to judge the harp much as they might a coloratura soprano--something of a musical oddity from whom they don't really expect much. Happily, the stigma may be ready to fall from both harp and coloratura.

The harp does not as readily compliment pure or abstract music as it might a ballade or poem. Whether this is the fault of the pure music available to the harp is a moot point. Sonatas have not been the harpists' forte.

As is pointed out in the earlier sections of this volume, the harp is the rightful joint heir to a great deal of the baroque and early classic keyboard music. Fear of the critics has gripped the hearts of all harpists who ever dared to program such music, so they have usually dropped it to stick to the old tried and true.

A lot of justifiable criticism has been leveled at the traditional harp repertoire. It has comparitively few pieces of really high quality. Our contention is that much of the older music composed for the harp has great worth and should be rediscovered and revived. Perhaps it is even true that as we have heard it said, "The true nature of harp music is the transcription."

Liszt certainly had no objections to transcriptions of his own or anybody elses music. As a matter of fact it seemed rather the common thing to do. Each performer played his own version or transcription of the music. Liszt himself even programmed his own transcription of the Beethoven Appassionata! As is evidenced by the letter quoted from Liszt to Posse, he really quite approved of the transcriptions of his Liebestraume for harp, and certainly endorsed the Parish-Alvars' transcription of the Chopin E Major Etude.

It may be that the evolution of harp music is following much the same pattern as piano music did, only a couple of generations late. The great quantity of pianists has naturally produced great volumes of piano literature. By far the great percentage of it is as bad as any music harpists have had to contend with, but there will also be a small percentage that is worthwhile.

There are relatively few harpists. The American Harp Society at this moment has many of them as members, but still their total membership is still less than one thousand. There may be about three thousand harpists in the U. S. who are at all active. Maybe five hundred earn more than a quarter of their income from playing, and probably less than fifty earn a full time livelihood from playing harp.

There has been an average of about eighty harps manufactured every year since 1900 in the United States. European production certainly did not total more than fifty harps per year until it virtually stopped altogether around 1930. Lyon Healy has supplied almost every harpist in the United states (except for around fourteen hundred harps made by Wurlitzer) and they recently began on serial number 5000. Simple addition totals about six thousand seven hundred harps made in the United States with some worn out, some destroyed and some second harps by the same harpist; we still can't come up with more than a maximum of five or six thousand people who own harps!

The astonishingly few harpists as compared to pianists (one quarter of a million new pianos are made every year in the United States) results in several problems. The volume of compositions for the harp is small, and even assuming that we get the same percentage of good music that pianists might, it would still not amount to more than one really good composition every two or three years. The finding of even these few then becomes another problem.

The best source of decent harp music today is, as it has always been, the harpist composer. This may be because the harpist usually puts out quite a lot of compositions, if they compose at all, and again our small percentage due to chance or whatever will give us at least a few that are good. The composer who is not a harpist may not write as many pieces for the instrument, but often the chances are that he will be a better composer, since his interest is great enough to lead him to compose for an instrument that is not his usual musical speech.

In writing critiques about harp music then, it would be wise and kind to keep in mind the quantity of quality that a harpist has to draw on and to encourage composers who show any promise at all. It would be just as wise to discourage those that clearly do not, but caution is advised. We recently got acquainted with two suites written for the harp by a fairly prominent foreign composer. The first in our opinion is not good and added nothing to the harp repertoire. We would have been slow in looking up other harp compositions by this man, but having the second suite in hand we did examine it. It was a charmer!--well written for the harp and altogether delightful!

Writing an opinion of a piece or a performer is a great responsibility. Unfortunately, it sometimes amounts to affecting public opinion to the point of failure or success for the individual, and this is in some cases more important to him than life or death.

The music we have discovered or rediscovered, Scarlatti, Bach, Haydn and the harp virtuosi, encourages us to hunt further. We also find that a typically small but important percentage of contemporary harp composition is showing definite signs of quality.

Harp music need not be a smashing bore, and we find many pieces of good music in disuse only because they are written in a form now out of style. For example, the theme and variations. Harp composers of about a century ago also had a habit of giving their compositions romantic titles that seem ludicrous to us now. Perhaps simply dropping the name, which might be, "Dance of the Fairies and Crickets" and calling it "Presto Leggiero" will help to redeem what otherwise may be an excellent composition.

A major problem of the harp in solo concert is that fact that it is more or less a chanber instrument, and a small chamber at that, and has a level of volume softer than most other instruments, thus requiring its listeners to work at listening every minute. The piano can, with its tremendous fortissimos, allow us to relax and not really listen closely for a moment once in a while. But with the poor harp, we must sit virtually on the edge of our chair, and the effect is tiring. A satisfactorily amplified harp is still somewhere in the future. It might even destroy the very nature of the harp's charm for it to be even a little bit louder.

It would be better then to judge the harp on the same basis of intimacy that one might judge a classic guitar recital, rather than a concert on a Steinway grand.

The critic will also gain much insight into the problems of the harpist by a thorough reading of the rest of this book.

The harp is a versatile

and useful instrument.

CHAPTER TWELVE: FOR THE CONDUCTOR

As we have suggested to the composer and the critic, we commend the rest of the volume to the conductor. A better appreciation of the problems facing his harpist will no doubt help to improve rapport between them, and perhaps also help with some of the necessary solutions.

THE PROBLEM OF PITCH

Tuning will always be a problem on the harp. The strings may go out of tune with the slightest change in humidity and temperature and both of these rise sharply during a concert. If possible, place the harp out of drafts in a position where such conditions will remain fairly constant. For the sake of overall intonation, the pitch of the orchestra should be rigidly held to a standard, with the least possible sharpening of the string section during a performance. Otherwise, you may choose whether to have the harp sharp during the first part, or flat during the last half.

Some orchestras make a special allowance to their harpist in order to keep good strings on the harp. This can amount to quite an expense during the year and may be found worth while to improve the sound from the harp section.

More and more orchestras are now purchasing their own harps. Pianos, celesta, percussion and other large instruments are maintained by the orchestra and owning a really fine harp is an excellent idea. Harpists may otherwise have to do all their practicing at the rehearsal hall or else move their own harp in and out for each rehearsal, both undesirable situations.

If space can be found, the harpist should be able to spend the large amount of time they are not·needed in rehearsals practicing. This is to the orchestra's benefit as well as their own. A dressing room or storage place is adequate as long as it is reasonably sound proof.

CUES

Harpists often have uncommonly long rests, and you will see them looking anxiously up at the conductor or at the tympani part or even the last desk second fiddles to find out where they are. A gradual understanding should arise after a while that a certain frown or smile from the conductor means "We have just reached letter J" or "Get ready, and I'll cue you."

CARRYING POWER

Individual harps will vary in the amount of carrying power they have. Though one may sound thin and small within twenty feet, the same harp may project a full and penetrating tone out to the audience. A routine check by the conductor or his assistant may ascertain how well it really does carry, and where it should be placed for the best tonal advantage. Placing the harp on a small riser or platform adds to the size of the tone since the platform will act as an additional sound-board.

PLACEMENT OF THE HARP IN THE ORCHESTRA

Placing the harps where they can be seen always pleases the harpists, but placing them where they can be heard will please the conductor. A wooden wall just behind the harps will project them even better than if they were on the very apron of the stage. As we have mentioned, a riser will help to project a harp, acting as additional soundboard material, and elevating the harp so that its sound is not absorbed by the clothing and players of the orchestra before it has a chance to project also helps. Keeping this in mind in placement, leaving space in front of the instrument will make it more audible.

SIGHT READING

We have decried loud and long in this volume the inability of today's harpist to sight read creditably, but we must point out in our own defense that sight reading on the harp entails certain special problems. Pedalling must usually be marked in some detail, particularly in modern music where the chromaticism becomes involved. With this done, half of the difficulty is eliminated, so let the harpist have the part as far in advance as possible. Otherwise expect them to have considerable difficulty for the first two or three times through.

AUDITIONS FOR A HARPIST

It is a nasty trick for a conductor to put the Magic Fire Music on the stand for a potential harpist to read for an audition. If the conductor wants to impress the harpist with his omniscience as to what is difficult for the harp and to embarrass the auditioner to the point of complete demoralization, it is a great piece to have them sight read. It will, however, prove nothing since even the best harpists who have this piece of Wagner coming up will use it as a warming up exercise for a couple of weeks before the concert.

We recommend that the conductor audition the harpist on the material that is standard in the orchestral repertoire with important harp parts, most of which is listed earlier in this volume under the Orchestral Harpist. This material, which every harpist should know before they attempt to play an audition, will let the conductor see what the harpist can do with preparation and from there how well they can alter their preconceived notions about the music in order to conform with the conductor's wishes as to tempos, dynamics, phrasing, and so on. This seems reasonable since most concerts are more or less prepared. As every conductor knows, experience counts for a great deal and especially so on the harp.

PRIOR ORCHESTRAL EXPERIENCE AND TRAINING

Unfortunately, most harpists are taught and trained more as if they were to become soloists rather than orchestral harpists. Even some of our finest conservatories and schools do not stress the learning of orchestral literature. Some even give very little orchestral experience. So it would be wise to watch for the harpist who has taken it upon himself to obtain and learn the standard harp parts from the orchestral repertoire. With the old war-horses under their fingers, there will be time to work out the new or difficult things that come up during the season.

A few harpists have also played other orchestral instruments, and these have very often made the best orchestral musicians, perhaps because phrasing can be learned better on a flute, for example, than on a piano or harp because of the necessity of breathing within the music. This and the probability of more previous ensemble playing may make them more valuable players. An instrumentalist who always plays alone is often thrown for a loss when he is required to fit in and blend with others.

WITH WHOM DID YOU STUDY?

No one teacher nor school of harp playing has actually produced consistently better harpists than any other. Primarily, one will notice differences in tone and repertoire, but little else will be audible. There will be greater differences brought about by the varying degrees of talent and temperment between any two harpists than there will be as a result of their particular school of playing. The place where they studied may make a greater difference because of the amount of orchestral experience possible. We feel it might be unwise to comment specifically on this since conditions may change, but certain schools do provide considerable more experience in ensemble playing than others.

ON TOUR

The harpist on tour with an orchestra has additional problems. Practice will be well nigh impossible unless special arrangements can be made. It will be worth a little extra trouble to have the harp unloaded first so that even fifteen minutes warm-up can be had. The special problems of moving and insuring harps are discussed elsewhere in this volume. Check them out. Back up the harpist in the demand for extreme care in handling. If a harp is broken on the road, there may be simply nothing that can be done about it.

HARPISTS ARE MUSICIANS, TOO

Expect your harpist to be a musician the same as the rest of the orchestra. They may be so surprised and pleased that they will work their heads off to prove to you that they are.

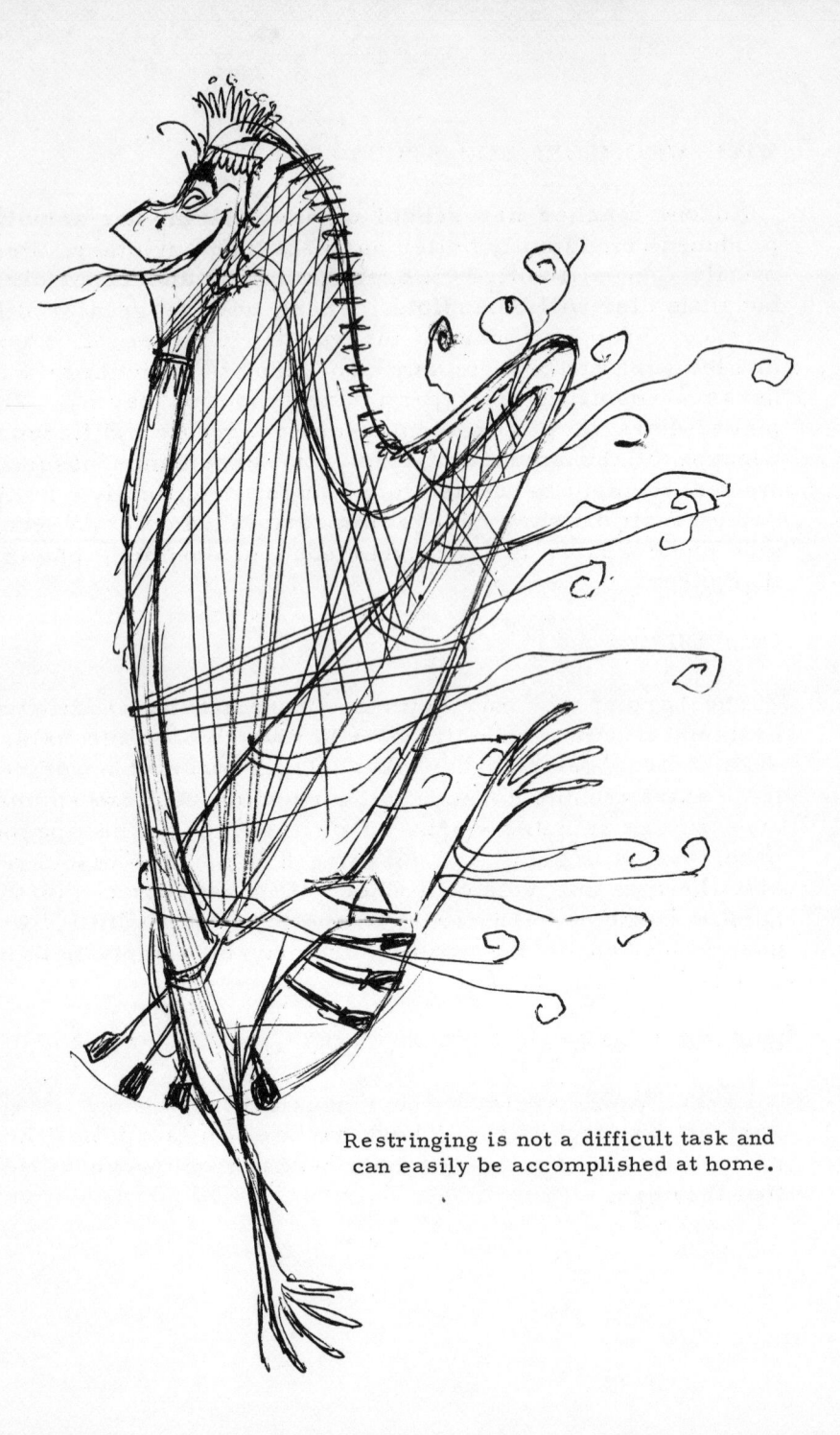

Restringing is not a difficult task and
can easily be accomplished at home.

CHAPTER THIRTEEN: STRINGING

In the ancient pyramid texts of Egypt, it is undoubtedly carved in stone that the best harps Isis ever made sound no better than the strings Thoth can make for them. The thought is still all too true.

NYLON VS. GUT

Basically, there are at present two types of strings available. Nylon and gut. There are varying qualities of both, and from observation, it appears that certain persons get better results with one kind while another gets the opposite.

Gut strings are made from the intestinal material of sheep but are called "catgut," which is as logical as most things today and is backed by long years of fine tradition. The material is broken down into long fibers which are then spun together with hide glue as a binder. The glue is water soluble and will break down with excessive perspiration or other moisture, fraying and ultimately breaking.

KEEP STRINGS CLEAN

Falseness is that quality in a string when it cannot vibrate consistently at a certain number of cycles per second, i.e. 440. This is because verying thicknesses or other factors such as dirt, causing the weight to vary from place to place along its length, will produce out of tune overtones, i.e. 877 instead of 880. In order to make the strings true after they have been spun, the final processor draws them through a diamond die to make certain that the string is the same diameter throughout its length. Since falseness may be caused by an accumulation of dirt, clean the strings with a soft cloth, but do not use water. Be careful in stringing in order to avoid a kink which will cause falseness especially in the larger gut strings.

Age alone will bring on falseness as the strings may stretch somewhat unevenly over a period of two or three years. Though a large string may sometimes give good service for many years longer, one or two years is considered excellent.

NYLON

Nylon strings have been in use on the harp since about 1948. They are considered by some as of inferior quality of tone, though many others prefer them. There can be little question that there is a difference in sound, but as to whether it is a better or worse quality can only be judged by what type of tone a person prefers. Scientifically speaking, the nylon string has more audible upper-partials and a very slightly longer ringing period. The greater richness in upper partials is recognized by some as the "tinnier" quality of nylons. This may actually be the very quality that would make them carry better.

A different manner of playing is required since the nylon string should not be plucked as vigorously. The same audible volume is obtained with less energy on the nylon and the sound may become distorted if a certain maximum is exceeded. Some harps respond better to nylons than do others, and all harps should be regulated for nylons when they are used as they respond slightly differently to the disc tension.

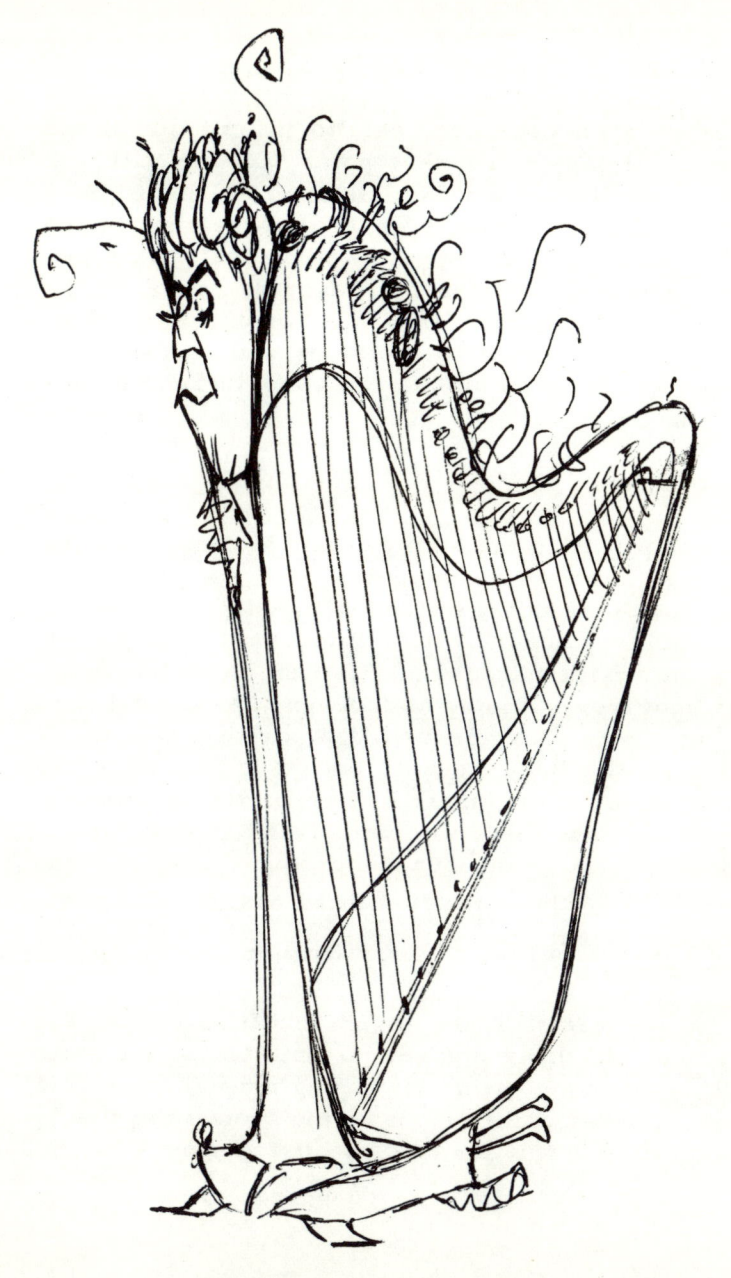

Some harpists sacrifice style and appearance for the sake of economy.

BETTER IN THE HIGHER OCTAVES

Generally the nylons are good only to the middle of the fourth octave. Strings below that point have up 'till now been made of a slightly too flexible type nylon and have weak tonal definition. There is general agreement in the use of nylon strings in the upper two octaves, since they rarely break and their greater brilliance is useful in the upper register of the harp. Breakage, or the lack of it, and the greater resistance to moisture and temperature pitch changes are responsible for an ever increasing acceptance of the nylon harp string.

THE TIE KNOT

The method of putting the string on the harp is much the same among all harpists and consists of a slip knot - see illustration - with the short end being the slip. In the upper three octaves insert a small piece of thicker gut string as a 'tie.' The purpose of this 'tie' is not so much to keep the knot from slipping up through the sound-board as to prevent a very sharp bend in the string where it is made into a knot. This prevents breakage at this point. Rolls of cotton, or even small rolls of tissue work at least as well and have the additional advantage of not buzzing against the back of the sound-board as a long string tie may sometimes do.

PULL THE HEAVY STRINGS TAUT BEFORE WINDING

The tie is not needed in the fourth and fifth octave, but it is important in these octaves to pull the string quite taut before beginning to wind the tuning pin. If the string is too loose, as it stretches it may wind around the tuning pin so many times that it presses against the neck of the

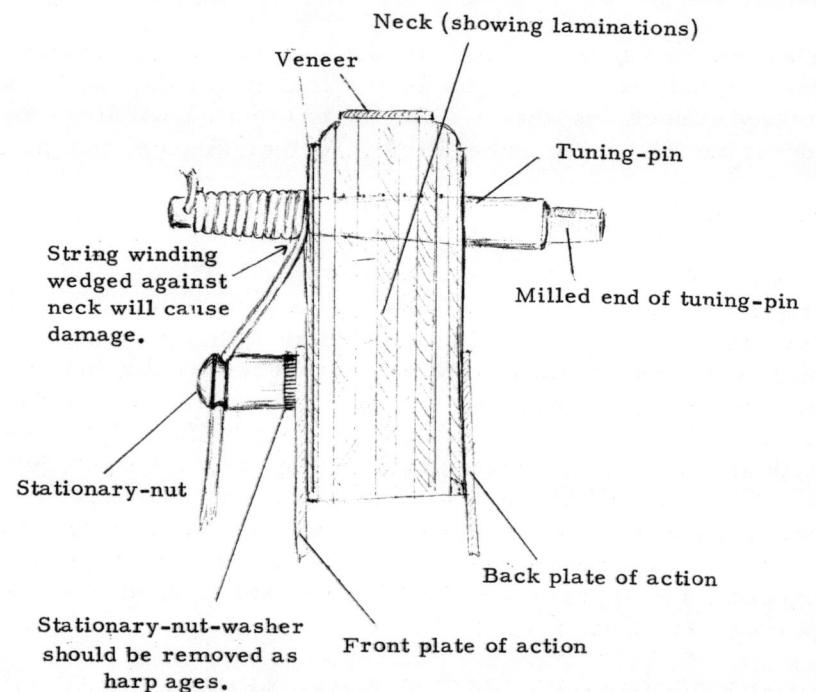

Neck (showing laminations)
Veneer
Tuning-pin
String winding wedged against neck will cause damage.
Milled end of tuning-pin
Stationary-nut
Back plate of action
Stationary-nut-washer should be removed as harp ages.
Front plate of action

The tie knot is as easy as

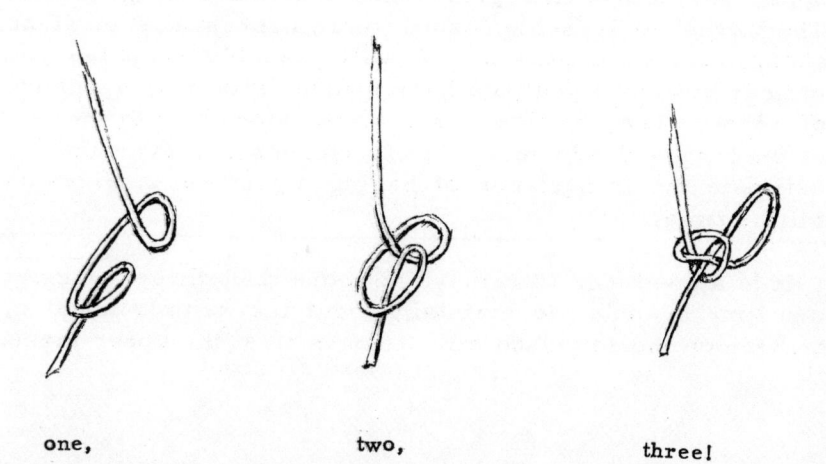

one,   two,   three!

harp and begins to pull the pin through the harp. Serious damage may result. If you have a tuning pin that is hard to turn, check for this. Take up the extra windings by loosening the string and pulling it farther through the pin.

NEED A TRIM?

It is not uncommon to see a harp that looks ready for a trip to the barber, with strings coiled or woven under and over the tuning pins. It is believed that this is an economy measure and that if the string breaks at the bottom, this extra length can then be put to use. Indeed, sometimes it can, but it will almost certainly be false from the kink and the uneven stretching. Strings dry out when left this way and will break sooner from it. Strings kept in a proper waxed envelope may last for years and be just as good as when they were new. Besides all the practical aspects, the appearance of an instrument is a clue to the players and their playing.

LEAVE SOME SLACK IN THE WIRES BEFORE WINDING!

Wire strings are a little more difficult to replace. They will go dead after about two years and loose the rich upper partials which give them their carrying power. They break only seldom and therefore usually must be changed for tonal reasons. It will probably surprise you to hear how good your old harp sounds with just a change of wires. They act as sympathetic vibrators to the rest of the harp and add much to its richness. Never underestimate the importance of having a good set of wires on all the time.

It is a good idea to remove no more than three wires at one time in order to maintain about the same amount of tension on the sound-board. Remove first the upper three,

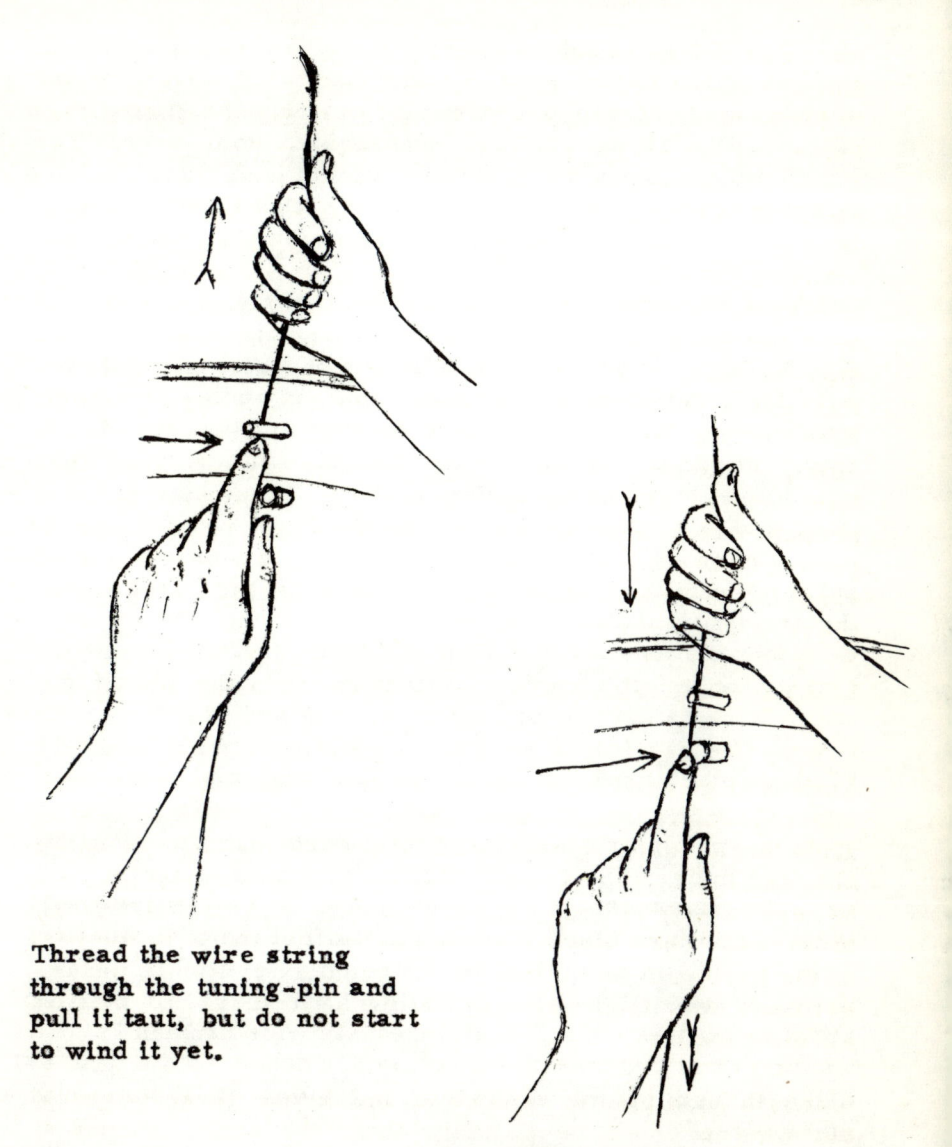

Thread the wire string
through the tuning-pin and
pull it taut, but do not start
to wind it yet.

Then slip it back about an inch
so there will be sufficient slack
for winding.

G, F and E, and replace them before continuing on down. Before trying to pull the old string out of the back of the sound-board, straighten or cut off entirely the curled part of the old wire so you will not scratch your harp. The wire cutters should be made for "music wire" and are obtainable from a good hardware store. Ordinary wire cutters may cut for a time, but will be quickly ruined.

Insert the new wire from the back of the board, pull it up completely taut through the tuning pin but DO NOT WIND YET! If you do, you will cut the string. Pull the wire taut, but then back it down about an inch - see illustration - so that you have about an inch of slack to wind around the pin. Now bend down the end of the wire so that it is kinked against the tuning pin; it will now stay in position, and you can wind the tuning pin. As you do, try to make the wire wind neatly and evenly around the pin by pulling the middle of the wire, taking up the slack. Pull the string immediately up to pitch even though it may continue to stretch and go flat for an hour or so. Cut off the extra wire length about one-half inch from the tuning pin. Extra wire can serve no useful purpose and may tear your cover. Be careful at all times. The core wire is of the hardest steel and can cause painful cuts and scratches.

Wire strings are made of a steel core wire with a winding of copper. The copper winding has been slightly plated with silver except on the Fs and Cs. This silver will tarnish and turn black, but will not affect the tone quality. Trying to clean or polish the wires only results in the removal of the light silver plating and they will remain about as dull as ever. The higher six wire strings have a winding of silk under the winding of copper. This acts to make the string more flexible and gives it a somewhat richer tone.

The wire strings must be inserted through
the openings in the rear of the harp.

STORING SPARE STRINGS

Most harpists keep at least one full set of spare strings on hand. Kept in their envelopes, spare strings will be good for years. A new harpist, however, can avoid the expense of keeping a lot of spares by having at least the F, A, A and E in each octave. The A will also do for the G and B, and the E can also be used for D. The F and C must be kept because of their different colors. Gauging strings will insure that the regulation is maintained. A replacement string of larger or smaller diameter will affect the disc tension, throwing the regulation out of tune. The string need not conform exactly to the gauge letter, and many harpists like a heavier or thinner string, but it should be as nearly consistent as possible. If you have new strings that vary from the gauge letter, simply remark them for their correct string size.

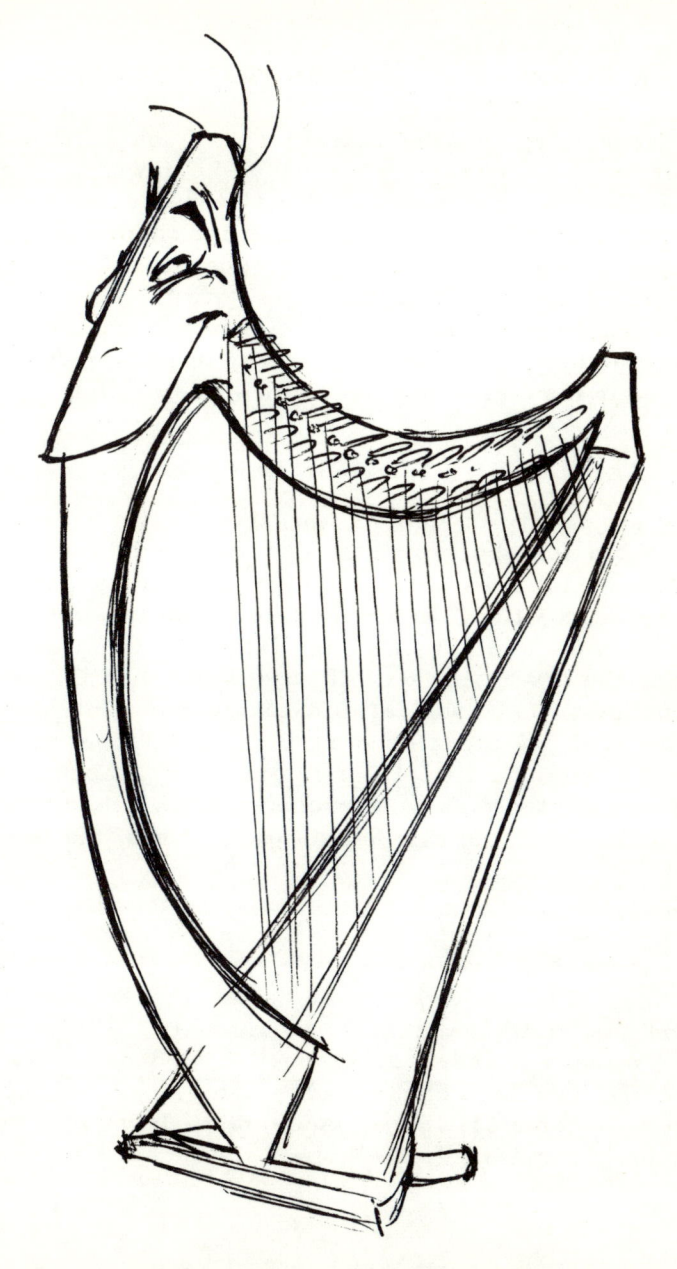

The Troubadour Harp is virtually worry-free.

CHAPTER FOURTEEN: TROUBADOUR TROUBLES

This little harp, on the market for such a little time, shows promise of changing the whole harp world, and indeed the life of every harpist. It may bring students coming to your door 'till you have no time for them. Many who have begun on the Troubadour have gone on with great ease and not missing a step to the pedal harp. This process will also increase the potential audience for concert harpists since audiences are often made up of non-professional or even poor players of the instrument they listen to.

BUZZES IN THE LEVERS

In its simplicity of design, the troubadour harp offers little trouble for the harpist. The most common is the slight buzz which may occur on a string with the lever up in the closed position. Early models of the troubadour had a brass stop pin against which the finger lever might buzz. In turning the lever, back it off slightly so that it does not touch the pin. This will eliminate the buzz and also improve the tone of the closed string. If this becomes too clumsy or slow, a little liquid latex, or rubber cement painted on the stop pins will probably help. Later models use a wooden pin, and this seems to get rid of the buzz.

REGULATION

The sharpening levers are made of a steel rod bent into a U shape. This allows for adjusting the tension of the lever on the string, and thus the intonation of the raised pitch. To make it sharper, widen the U bend, to lower it squeeze the two legs of the U closer together. If the tuning levers become too loose, take out the lever and work a little rubber cement into the hole, this should tighten it up without making it too difficult to turn. If it is still too loose, take out the lever and flatten out the end slightly and tap it back into the neck.

The sound-board is a laminated birch and will never pull up. The necks seem to show no sign of twisting, so there is not much else to go wrong other than real damage, and it takes quite a lot to hurt a troubadour. Repairs can be made at the factory or by a qualified cabinet maker.

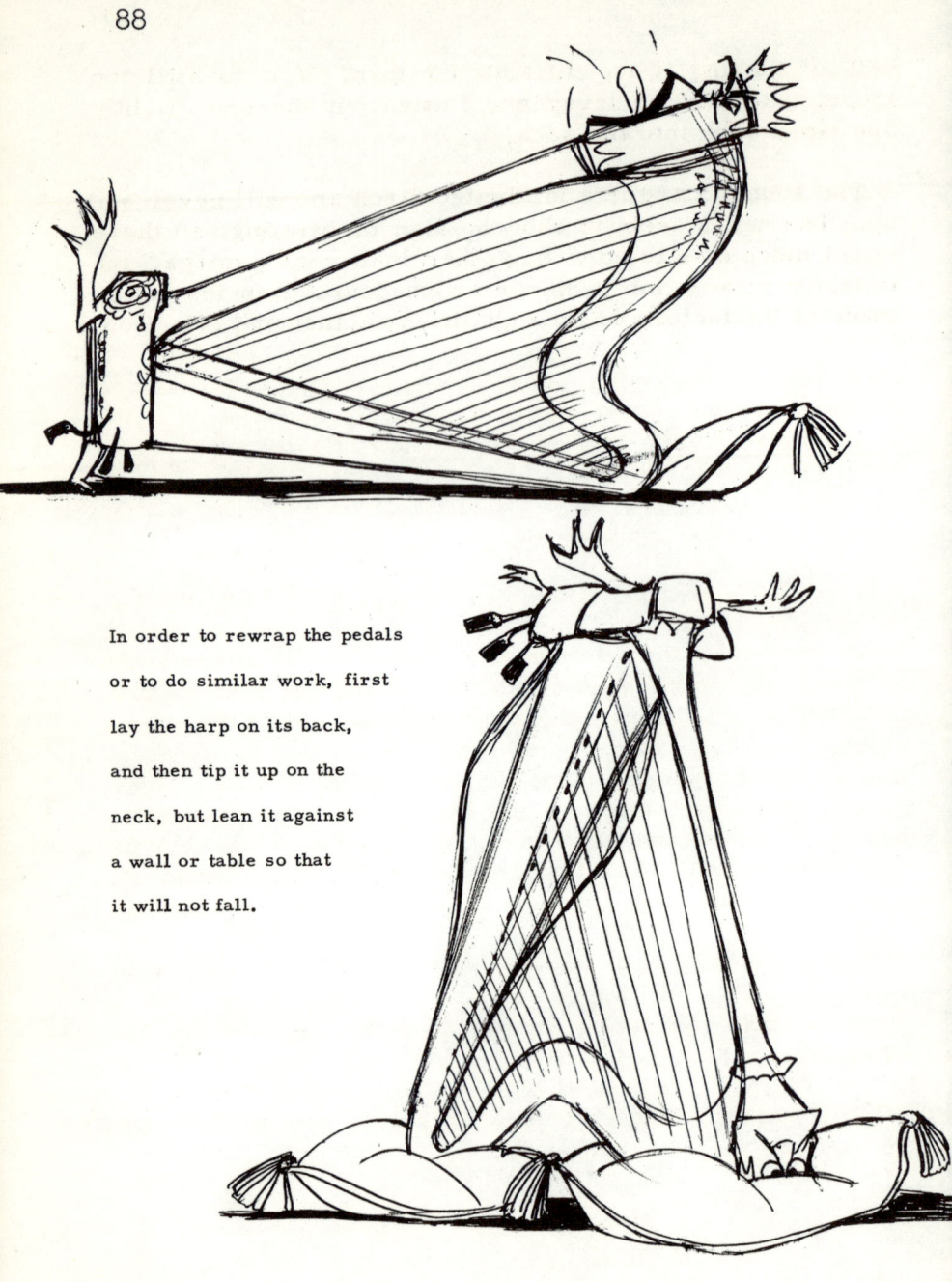

In order to rewrap the pedals or to do similar work, first lay the harp on its back, and then tip it up on the neck, but lean it against a wall or table so that it will not fall.

CHAPTER FIFTEEN: WRAPPING THE PEDALS AND REPLACING THE CAPS

As a rule the pedal felts should be changed about once a year. A busy harpist though may find they will have to be done as often as every three months. There are two reasons. They may be worn through, or they may be packed down. In either case they reduce the distance of the pedal from the body of the harp, and this has a critical effect on the regulation of the instrument. In a harp that has not even been played, the pedal springs will exert enough pressure to pack down the felt by 1/16th of an inch with deleterious effects on the regulation. Foam rubber inserts pack down even faster with the same results.

CHANGING THE FELTS

It will be easier to change the felts with the harp upside down. Lay it first on its body. The rear feet will still touch the floor, and a pillow or rug that won't slip should be placed under the knee-block. Then lift the base so that the harp is resting on the neck and the top of the knee-block. Take care to have something to protect the neck on the floor, and lean the harp against a table or wall. Make sure it can't slip! Remove the base by the four base bolts which are unscrewed with your tuning key. They may be left in the base so that they will not get lost or mixed up. Sometimes they are different lengths. If they are, the shortest goes in front, the longest in back. Remove the spring if you can, and only one at a time, or if you would rather leave it on, the pedal can be propped up with a spool so that you can work on the felt. Remove the old wrapping.

Felts are obtainable in sets of seven, precut for the

90

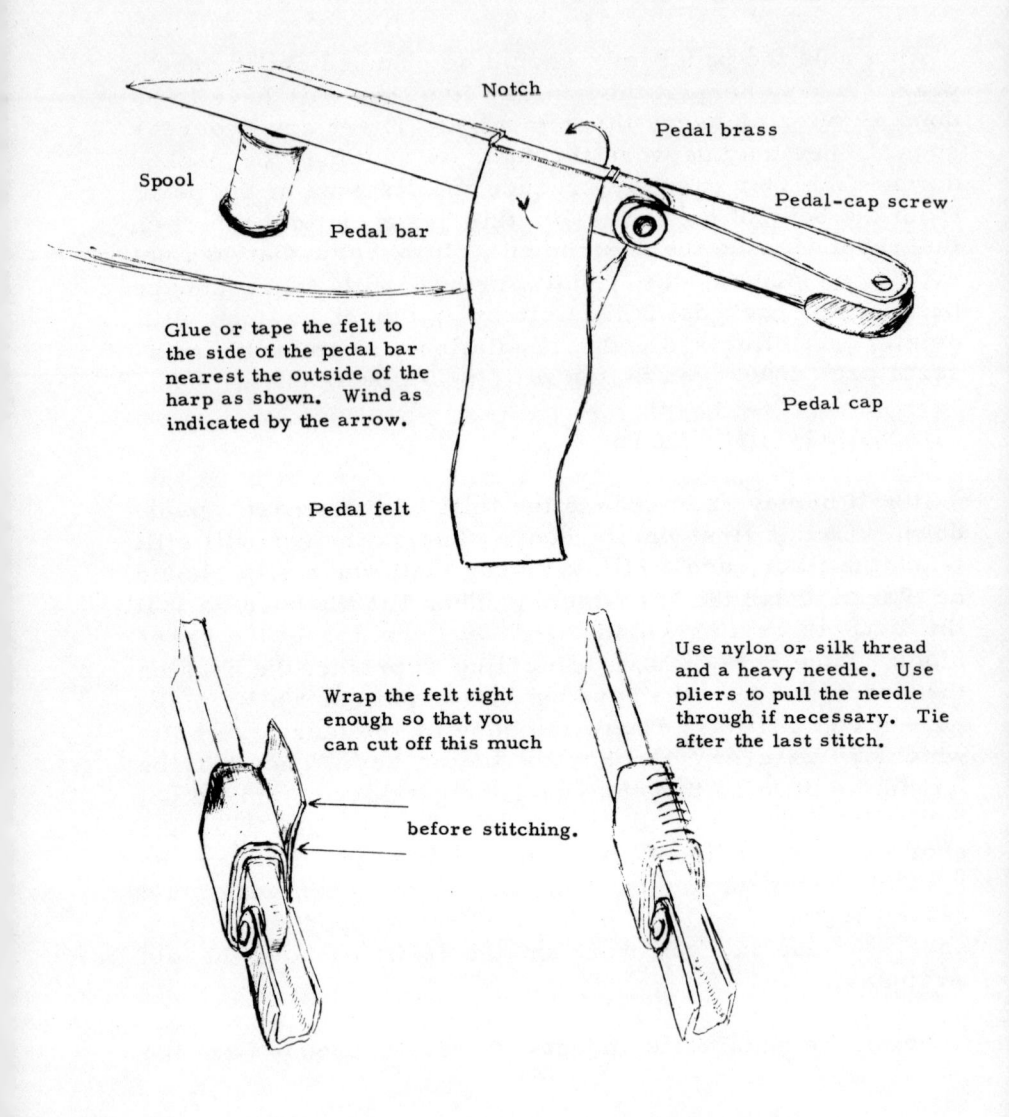

Spool

Notch

Pedal brass

Pedal-cap screw

Pedal bar

Glue or tape the felt to the side of the pedal bar nearest the outside of the harp as shown. Wind as indicated by the arrow.

Pedal cap

Pedal felt

Wrap the felt tight enough so that you can cut off this much

before stitching.

Use nylon or silk thread and a heavy needle. Use pliers to pull the needle through if necessary. Tie after the last stitch.

correct width and length. The material is not really ordinary felt, but a highly expensive bushing cloth which is used in piano manufacture. It is a woven facric which has also been felted and is extremely durable. Ordinary felt used on the pedals would last less than a month.

With a small piece of scotch tape, fix one end of a strip of felt to the pedal bar. Let it hang down from the side of the pedal which is closest to the outside of the harp, i. e. left pedals on the left side, right on the right side. The upper end of the felt should be even with the upper edge of the pedal bar. See illustration. Wind it around the bar. It should pass through and fill a slot in the bar just the width of the felt. Make the winding as tight as possible, twisting it still more so that you are able to cut off about 1/2 to 3/4 of an inch before sewing. See illustration. Use a heavy needle and heavy nylon or silk thread, a good thimble and a pair of small pliers. Waxing the thread with beeswax makes it easier also. Replace the spring before going on.

Remember that the winding must be done in opposite directions on the two sides of the harp. Make sure that you start with the felt in the correct position, and you will find it difficult to go wrong. A lot of fancy stitches are not necessary; between six and eight will do nicely. When you are finished, replace the base, fitting the pedals into the proper slots, and make sure the small base pins fit into the correct holes. Replace the base bolts and tighten them firmly, but not too tight. Tighten them too much and you will damage your harp.

With the harp in this upside down position, it is a simple matter to replace the pedal caps. Simply unscrew the small screw on the upper side of each pedal, fit a new cap on and screw it up tight. These screws must be really tight. Ninety-five percent of all buzzes comes from these little beasts when they are too loose. It is sometimes economical to switch pedal caps from one side of the harp to the other since they usually wear only on the one side. The saving may be small, but it is a neat trick to know, when your feet are slipping off the pedals and you don't have any new caps.

Intonation should never be a problem on the harp since the instrument is easily kept in tune by the performer.

CHAPTER SIXTEEN: TUNING

Tuning is often a most disorganized process with a harpist, so we are inserting this section, hopefully, to present a little of the theory, and a pretty sound version of the practice.

THE HARP IS A TEMPERED INSTRUMENT

The harp, like the piano and organ, is necessarily a tempered instrument, since the pitch of a given note cannot be tuned during the process of performing. It is true that the harp has different strings for enharmonic unisons, i.e. D# and Eb. This has led some to think that a harp can be regulated for "just" intonation such as would be played by a violin. If D# or Eb or any other note were always the same pitch in all keys it would be possible, but unfortunately, such is not the case.

With perfect or "just" intonation, two interesting mathematical phenomena are readily apparent. First, the frequency of say A-440 cps. is doubled for the same note an octave higher, i.e. A-880. Second, the frequency is increased by half its value for the fifth higher. A-440 then would be perfectly in tune to E-660. But lack-a-day, in turning to our table of computed tempered frequencies, we find that if A is 440 cps., the E fifth above is 659.26 instead of 660 cps. What happened to our other 74 thousandths of a vibration!?

MATHEMATICAL DEMONSTRATION

Let us for once and all go through the complete cycle of twelve tones, computing each value from A-440, multiplying by one and a half (1.5) for the fifth above, or three quarters (.75) for the fourth lower:

Now it is apparent that if fourths and fifths are perfectly tuned, each has become progressively sharper until upon completing the cycle our original A is now almost six vibrations sharp!

Therefore, in a given key, each note of the scale must be tuned in relation to the root tone. Thus, C# in the key of A tuned perfectly with the A will be 550 cps. a number that is mathematically consonant with both A-440 and its perfect fifth E-660 making a smooth beat-free triad. However, C# tuned perfectly to the key of D, even though the D is perfectly consonant with the A-440 will be of a different pitch than the C# we had in the key of A!

THE DISCREPANCY IS GREATER FOR MORE REMOTE KEYS

The mathematical discrepancy becomes even wider when the common tone between two keys is not the tonic; for example, the keys of Eb and A have D natural in their scales. Even though we make the two Ds the same pitch exactly, the other common tones with different names, i. e., G# and Ab will be out of tune.

We hope that from the above demonstration it is quite apparent that the tempered scale is the best solution to freedom of modulation through all the keys, and we find strength in recalling that Bach thought so, too.

A PRACTICAL AND ACCURATE METHOD OF TUNING

Believing and doing are often too widely separated, so how is such a tempered scale obtained in actual practice? The most accurate and satisfactory way is to tune in fourths and fifths while setting the temperment. This must be the first octave tuned, and greatest accuracy can be obtained by tuning from middle or fourth octave C. This is because a lower register allows you to count the beats and judge temperment more easily, and the key of C will make for less error if your harp is slightly out of regulation.

WHAT ARE BEATS?

When two strings which should be at the same pitch are not, for example, one at A-440 and the other at A-442, a phenomenon occurs commonly called beats or waves. Between these two tones there would be two beats per second, or 442 minus 440, which is not very much. If a fifth is out of tune, one string at A-440 and the other E-657 there will be three beats per second, because as you will remember reading above, the E should be 660 cps. to be perfectly in tune.

If you have trouble hearing beats, practice listening for them by tuning your C# and Db perfectly and lowering one of the pitches slowly, counting the speed of the beats as they increase. Then do the same sort of thing with an octave, a fifth, and all the other intervals until you recognize and hear beats easily. A good ear is not really necessary for good tuning, only the ability to count.

Again we have over simplified. Hearing beats on the harp is difficult since the tone decays and fades so quickly.

In tempering fourths and fifths, the tone fades so rapidly that rather than actually being able to count the very slow beats you will have to feel a quality of out-of-tune-ness. When two tones are only slightly out of tune with only one or two beats per second, it is slmost impossible to determine which tone is higher or lower except by moving it. This makes it possible to err so that a fifth will be tuned too wide rather than slightly narrow. Using the check indicated will almost always help to spot this type of error before you have gone so far as to throw the entire temperment off.

THE METHOD

Tune 4th C to the standard pitch. A 'C' tuning fork of 523.25 cps., which sounds an octave above 4th C will be in temperment with A-440 and is what you want. Orchestras being what they are, and string players even more so, it will be best to tune two or three beats sharp. This will put your harp at about A-442. Follow the outlined procedure indicated below:

Follow the outlined procedure on the staff. It is arranged so that in order to temper the fourths and fifths wider and narrower, respectively, each note is tuned slightly flat, except for the two Fs which must be tuned slightly sharp.

Tune 4th F to C; then tune 4th G to C; tune 4th D to the G. Now check the interval F and D. If you have tuned your fourths slightly wide, and the fifth slightly narrow, you should have beats in the F-D interval at the rate of about eight per second. This is correct, so proceed. Tune the 4th A to the D and check F and A, which should have beats slightly slower than the F-D or about seven per second. Now tune the 4th E to the A and check G-E. It should have about nine beats per second, and C-E should have about ten beats per second. In this order check F-A, F-D, G-E, C-E; they should increase the speed of their beats in the ratio of 7, 8, 9 and 10 per second. Now tune the B to the E, and check G-B which should have beats at about seven and one half per second, or just faster than F-A, and just slower than F-D.

TEMPERED OCTAVE SETS CORRECT RELATIONSHIPS

Bravo! You have just set your temperment! All the rest of the harp must be tuned to this octave in order to have the proper relationship. Tune down through the lowest part of the harp before tuning the upper strings. Tune E 5th to E 4th; D 5th to D 4th; and so on. The reason for tuning the lowest strings first is because of their high tension; as they are adjusted, they will throw the lighter upper octaves out if they have been tuned first.

CHECK CONSTANTLY

As you tune downward in octaves, also check in twelfths, and octave and a fifth, and in tenths. There should be quite a noticable beat in the tenths, but should still sound good, and the speed of the beats should decrease as you get lower. The twelfths should be almost perfectly smooth. Octaves are to be tuned perfectly, except as you descend into the base they must be stretched slightly wider to compensate for the human ear which will hear them as being sharp when played loudly. A corresponding correction should be made in the extreme treble, stretching the octaves slightly wider to compensate for the ear which will hear the high notes as flat! Do not over do this, your own ear will tell you when it sounds right, and probably you will make the correction automatically without trying for it.

CHECK AND RECHECK, ESPECIALLY THE TEMPERED OCTAVE

After all the wires are tuned, recheck the temperment octave, and then proceed on up, tuning the upper octave to the lower. Check in fifths, fourths, tenths, twelfths and chords. Never tune a lower octave to an upper, except of course below the temperment octave, in which case never tune an upper octave to a lower! Never tune one of the notes of your temperment octave to any other octave, but always recheck and correct the temperment. Just staying organized and following these rules will save a lot of time and greatly improve your tuning.

CHAPTER SEVENTEEN: REGULATING THE ACTION

Before beginning any regulation work on your harp read this chapter all the way through carefully at least twice, and make sure you understand it. Procedures merely mentioned in the first part, or theory of regulation, will be explained in more detail later, so read on! Read on!

Do not try to regulate your harp until you have made certain that it has a good set of felts on. If they are worn or packed down, you will be wasting your time and causing yourself a good deal more work anyway. Simply rewrapping the pedals will often take care of most regulation problems since the pedal will be restored to its proper position, and thus the closure of the disc will be corrected. With good felts on, the pedal rods are the next to be checked for correct adjustment. But, as mentioned above, this will be explained below.

It is almost impossible to regulate a harp perfectly without some electronic assistance. The Stroboconn and Strobotuner offer a method of regulating for a perfect half-step and no other method has been found that is nearly as accurate on the harp. The piano has full use of twelve semi-tones and can therefore be cross-checked as needed for accuracy, but the harp, with only seven of the twelve tones in our scale, can not. Therefore, the best full regulation can be made only when electronic assistance is available. Minor regulations, however, must be made quite often and a harpist who can't take care of these simpler maintenance problems is at a serious disadvantage.

HOW FAR IS A HALF-STEP?

A few words about theory may be of help, provided they do not frighten the hopeful harpist away. The length, the weight, and the tension of the vibrating string determine the pitch. Given any three of these four factors (length, weight, tension and pitch) the other can be computed. On the harp, once a string is stretched in the open position, its weight and length are constant; varying the tension by means of the tuning-pin will then change the pitch which is, of course, how a harp is tuned. The lute makers of the middle ages discovered in placing the frets on the neck of a lute that if they shortened the open string by 1/18th of its length, it would raise the pitch precisely one half-tone. This even allows for the slight change in tension caused by pressing down the string. This rule applies to the harp also.

EACH DISC MUST SHORTEN THE STRING BY 1/18th

Thus, if the open string is eighteen inches long, the upper disc must be placed so that the lower pin of the disc will be exactly one inch below where the string passes over the nut, and so shorten the string by one inch, or 1/18th of its length. For the moment, the lower or sharpening disc will be ignored, and we shall concern ourselves with only the upper or naturalizing disc. As a harp ages, the sound-board is pulled up. This is due to the nature of the wood, and though it happens faster in some harps than others, it appears to be an inevitable process. As the board is pulled up, the string length is shortened, sometimes quite considerably. Indeed, an eighteen inch string may be shortened by an inch or more on an old harp. But consider now what has happened to our regulation.

IF THE BOARD IS PULLED UP, THE DISCS SHORTEN THE STRING TOO MUCH

The disc set to shorten the string by one inch, or 1/18th

or its length, still shortens the string by one inch, but this inch is now greater than 1/18th of the string length. It now shortens the string by 1/17th, and consequently, raises the pitch somewhat more than the desired half-tone. So the pitch is too sharp with the disc closed, but correct regulation is easily accomplished by simply lowering the adjustable nut 1/18th of an inch (in the case of our imaginary eighteen inch string). This would make the distance from the adjustable nut to the bottom disc pin 17/18th of an inch, and again we are shortening the string by 1/18th of its total length, and our intonation should be correct.

CENTER THE STRINGS

As you are now prepared to find out, this is a gross over-simplification. We do have a second disc to worry about. The string, besides being shortened by the pulling up of the board, is also displaced forward toward the column (usually). The adjustable nut must be moved back toward the knee-block, to bring the string as near as possible into the center of the disc. This is not too difficult when we have only the top disc to consider, but we now find that it is only the lower end of the string which has been displaced toward the column, and this puts it on an angle so that it can't be centered in both discs. What do you do? Compromise, and do the best you can. It is preferable, generally speaking, to center the string more in the lower disc than the upper, since playing the string fortissimo may cause it to touch one of the disc pins as it is plucked making an objectionable although slight buzz. By watching carefully as the string is pulled out of vertical, you can see if it touches the disc pins. Usually it will touch only the lower pin, but if properly centered it can be played as loudly as desired without buzzing.

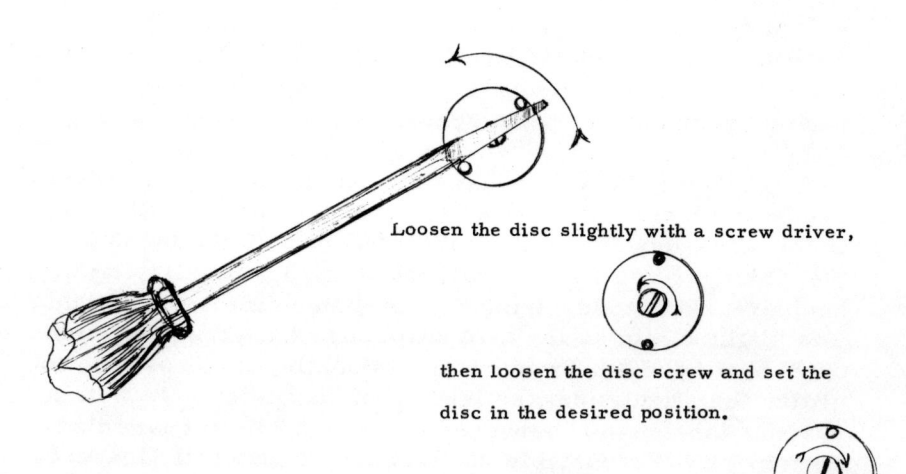

Loosen the disc slightly with a screw driver, then loosen the disc screw and set the disc in the desired position.

Tighten the disc screw.

ADJUST THE LOWER DISC BY VARYING THE TENSION

Let us now consider the lower or sharpening disc. The distance between the adjustable nut and the natural disc can be adjusted as shown above, the the distance between the two discs is not variable. The pitch can now be corrected only by adjusting the tension of the disc gripping the string. The tighter the disc, the sharper the half-step. Since the distance between the two discs will be more than the required 1/18th, with our pulled-up sound-board, the half-step will always be too sharp. (It might be noted here that harps still have personalities, and the author has upon occasion, in violation of all the rules, found an old harp flat in the sharpened position; so you must still depend on your ear and good sense.)

By reducing the grip of the disc on the string the pitch can be lowered. Often when the board is badly pulled up, it is necessary to compromise and reduce the tension of the upper disc so that the natural string is slightly flat to keep the sharpened string from being impossibly high. Too slight a grip by the disc will cause the string to buzz or at best have a poor tone. Occasionally, it is possible to utilize the slight sidewise leeway of the adjustable nut in varying the tension between the nut and the upper disc. By moving the adjustable nut forward it generally lessens the tension of the upper disc and may be helpful in bringing the lower disc into correct pitch. Conversely, moving the adjustable nut back will increase the tension and make the natural a little higher.

EXACT REGULATION MAY NOT BE POSSIBLE

It is probably becoming apparent from reading this chapter, even without working on a harp, that it may not be possible to correct the regulation. What then? This is often completely impossible to regulate a harp because the board is pulled up too high. Most of the time, however, it is possible to make some improvement and though the regulation may not be perfect, it will get by "just one more season."

With a good grasp of the above, the harpist should be able to recognize why a harp needs regulation. The sound-board may be pulled up. The pedal felts may be worn or packed down. Or in a new harp, especially, the action may be settling into position, that is, the tension of the discs on the strings causes them to be forced back, and this must be corrected and tightened at the "1,000 mile first year check-up."

VARIOUS METHODS OF CORRECTING THE REGULATION

The harpist should recognize the methods of correction. Usually, the adjustable nut must be lowered slightly to compensate for a pulled-up-board. The adjustable nut must be moved forward or back to center the string with the lower disc. The tension of the discs must be adjusted to correct the intonation of the lower or sharpening disc, often with a compromise. Care must be taken to make certain that the disc is not made so loose as to spoil the tone or to buzz. The lower gut strings and all the wires do not have adjustable nuts, but instead have stationary nuts. Thus, any regulation on these strings is done entirely by disc tension. Fortunately, the length of these strings is long enough so that the rise in the sound-board is a small fraction of the total string length and has only slight effect on their regulation. The most noticeable problem on these strings is the loss of grip by the discs caused by worn or thin pedal felts and is, of course, immediately corrected by changing the felts. The celluloid tubes covering the disc pins for the wire strings may become loose or worn. They can sometimes be rotated half a turn giving a new surface to the string. Replace them by unscrewing the old tube; tap the new one almost all the way on, and then screw it the rest of the way. Do not pinch them with pliers or they will become loose and buzz.

The above, we hope, has been a thorough discussion of what to do and why, but so far we have not detailed exactly how. That now follows.

REGULATING THE PEDAL RODS

When it is certain that you have a good set of felts on the harp, (see section on changing felts) next check the pedal rods for over-movement. This is done by putting the pedal into the middle or natural notch and then slowly moving it into sharp. Watch the upper or natural disc carefully to make sure that it does not move and grip the string any tighter. This upper disc, once the movement into natural has been completed, should grip the string and remain virtually motionless while the lower completes its movement. If the upper disc does move, it may be gradually forced into a clock-wise direction by the string and will ultimately result in a slightly open disc causing a most disagreeable buzz particularly in the wire strings.

To correct over-motion in the natural disc, the effective length of the pedal rod must be shortened. With the harp column down on a table and the base removed, unscrew the coupler screw from the coupler and pedal bar.

107

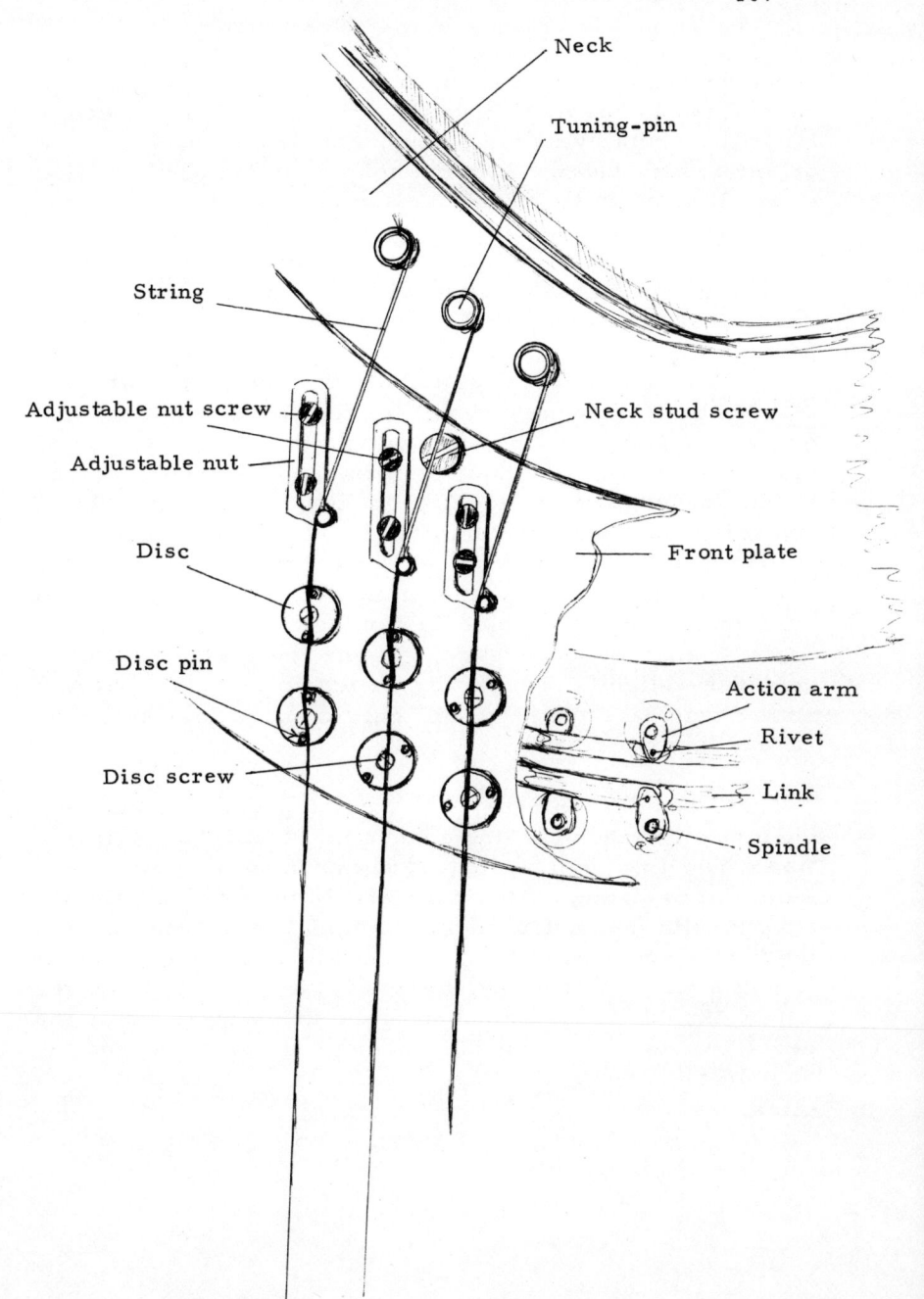

Turn the coupler two or three turns clock-wise and be careful not to cut your fingers. On new harps the couplers cut from cylindrical steel are sharp; use a screw driver to turn them. With the coupler in the new position fasten it again to the pedal bar and check it for over motion. This entails a lot of work replacing the base, etc., but is necessary. The E and F rods can be adjusted without removing the base, and with an extremely long thin screw driver you may find it possible to adjust the other pedals without removing the base by working the screw driver through the pedal slots. At any rate, you can fasten the base with only two of the four bolts while the test process is going on and save a little time. If the natural disc still moves, take another turn, and re-check. If you screw the coupler on too far, making the rod too short, you will incur two problems; first, it will be difficult to get the pedal down into the sharp notch, and second, the disc will not open wide enough in flat, and the string will buzz against the disc pins in fortissimo. Again, a compromise may be necessary. If the natural disc moves only very slightly, it may be better to leave it that way rather than have the pedal difficult to move into sharp or have a disc too closed.

The E pedal often creates a special problem since this chain has the shortest link connecting it with the main action. You may feel a sort of hump in moving the pedal from flat to sharp. This hump should be made to coincide exactly with the natural notch. Regulating the coupler on the rod is a fine point here and occasionally must be exact to half a turn. Generally, however, the pedal rod coupler screw should always be put in from the same side of the pedal bar as you found it, since the screw shank and the hole in the pedal bar are slightly tapered to prevent a click.

POSITIONING THE ADJUSTABLE NUT

When the over-motion is gone or reduced to a minimum, center the strings as nearly as possible or practical by moving the adjustable nut forward or back. To reposition an adjustable nut, use a screw driver of the correct size to fit the two small screws in the adjustable nut slot. Use enough pressure to make sure your screw driver will not slip out of the screw slot and spoil the screw. Turn both screws counter-clock-wise one revolution. This should make the adjustable nut easy to move. If you find it easier with the string removed, it is not necessary to lower the tension, just lift it off the nut by pushing the string forward with your thumb pointed down.

You will recall, (if you don't, reread the beginning of this section) that when the board is pulled up, the string is shortened and a corresponding correction must be made by lowering the adjustable nut to bring the natural down to pitch. The adjustable nut must also be positioned so as to bring the string into the center of the lower disc screw. With the nut in the new correct position, hold it with the thumb of one hand, and with the other, firmly tighten the two small screws. Do not force them, they can break or strip the threads in the brass plate. However, if they are not tight enough they may cause a slight buzz, so make them firm, but just don't force.

CENTERING THE STRING

When centering a string, it is necessary to check with the string on. If you can't get the string in the center, it may be possible if you file the slot in the adjustable nut a little wider, or even file the groove in the nut itself a little deeper. In either case take the adjustable nut completely off the harp. Use a small enough file, and be neat and careful. Make sure you polish away all the rough edges or they will cut the string. Emery cloth torn into 1/16 inch strips is good for smoothing. On stationary nuts in the bass, the strings must be centered by filing the grooves in the nuts, but remember when you file parts, they may have to be replaced when a new neck or board is put on and will add to the expense. If you can get by without drastic measures, it is better that way.

Wire strings should be centered carefully since they will make a sizzle as the disc is closed or opened if they are out of center. The stationary nut must be filed to bring them back, or changed to a larger or unfiled nut to move them forward. With a badly pulled board, accurate centering of the strings may not be possible.

RAISING AND LOWERING THE PITCH

The pitch of a note may be raised or lowered by varying the disc tension of the string. To adjust the tension of a disc, first loosen the disc by placing the blade of a screw driver between the disc pins and turning slowly counter-clock-wise; place the disc in the new desired position and tighten the screw clock-wise. To make a note sharper, increase the tension or grip of the disc by repositioning it slightly in a counter-clock-wise direction; then, tighten the screw, clock-wise. When it is closed, it will hold the string more tightly, thus raising the pitch slightly. The tension of the string may force the disc back a little, so position it just slightly tighter than you actually want it.

Tighten the screw barely firmly at first, and the discs can be positioned more exactly in either direction by using the blade of the screw driver as a lever. Close the disc on the string by means of the pedal, and then adjust its exact tension and pitch with the screw driver between the pins. When it is correct, put the pedal up and tighten the screw firmly. Never force any screw or disc. Never change anything that you cannot put back just like it was. Broken parts may not be a complete disaster, but they can be a nuisance, and they can cost you time and money.

Broken screws, when they occur and you can't get them out yourself, can be removed by a good locksmith. Additional help can usually be had from a good machinist. There is one in almost every town. Check the yellow pages for a machine shop.

LOWERING THE STRING PITCH

When it is necessary to lower the pitch of a string, which is usually the case in the sharp discs, reduce the tension of the disc by moving it clockwise with the blade of your screw driver. You may be able to do this in the upper register without loosening the screw, but be careful. You can break the screw or the disc by too much pressure. Never try to move it this way more than a little way. If it doesn't turn with just a little pressure, you will have to loosen the disc screw by first loosening the disc as outlined above, reposition it and tighten the screw, but not so firmly that you cannot make the final adjustment with the screw driver and, of course, your own good ear. When it is correct, tighten the screw more firmly.

OVER-SIZE DISCS

To lower the pitch of the highest five or six notes in sharp is sometimes almost impossible. Over-size single pin discs have been made that may help this. Being oversize, the single pin closes higher on the string and thus makes a smaller half-step so that it will not be quite as sharp. This is effective only in the sharp row. Over-size discs in the natural row would only increase the error as would over-size discs anywhere else on the harp. On double pin discs a smaller than standard might serve to bring down an over-sharp tone, but this would also increase the possibility of buzzing on the more closely spaced disc pins and make centering the string critical.

In the natural discs, lowering the pitch is easiest by lowering the adjustable nut. Loosen the screws and slide it down, often as far as it will go, if your harp is an old one. Check the string to make sure that it is still centered with the bottom disc; hold the adjustable nut in position with one hand and tighten the screws with the other.

COMPROMISE

You will find that on old harps most of the time you must compromise with a natural that is slightly flat and a sharp which is slightly sharp, and the sharp discs will often be so sharp that the disc tension cannot be loosened enough to bring the note down to pitch without spoiling the tone or indeed allowing the string to buzz.

A loose screw may cause a slight buzz.

CHAPTER EIGHTEEN: BUZZES, BURRS, FLUTTERS AND RATTLES

These can be the most exasperating part of repairing a harp. Buzzes often sound as if they are coming from one place and actually are from another part of the harp altogether, or sometimes even from an object in the room. Always check this last possibility first by taking the harp somewhere else and trying it.

Most buzzes are caused by the little pedal cap screws on the underside of the pedals. Check these first and make sure they are as tight as you can get them. Next, check the front and rear feet screws. Once in a while it will not be possible to tighten these screws since metal and wood will never remain tight together forever. If the screw won't tighten and keeps turning in the wood, take it out and put two or three little pieces of heavy maple tooth picks and some Elmer's glue into the hole. Now put the screw back in and give it a couple of hours to dry; then tighten it up.

A BUZZ IS USUALLY A LOOSE SCREW

If the buzz is still with you, go over the harp carefully and tighten every screw you can find. If you have the new type of back-plate screws with the lock-nut on them, tighten the nut rather than the screw. Don't forget the screws in the handle and the crown. How about the strings and string ties inside the body of the harp? Try holding them one at a time or moving them slightly while trying for the buzz. Maybe those strings you have wound around the neck of the harp are causing the buzz. Trim them off; they will look much better anyway. Did you try all the little screws on the adjustable nuts? The disc screws are always tightened automatically, and so are almost certainly not the problem. Leave them alone.

Try placing a finger lightly on each disc as you play for the buzz. If you find that one of these stops the buzz, take off the back-plate screw and put another little steel washer in it. If you have the new type of back-plate screws, give it a quarter turn clock-wise. This will tighten the pressure the back-plate spring exerts on the spindle shank against the front plate which may be buzzing. Do not tighten the back-plate screws indiscriminately, or you may find you have your action so tight it won't move.

BUZZES SOMETIMES IN THE WOOD

If none of these stops the buzz, it may be in the wood somewhere, especially if it comes and goes on humid or dry days. Try pushing down on the center-strip to see if there is a section that has come loose from the board. This would have to be fixed by working a little glue, preferably clear epoxy, underneath. It is a difficult job, and not to be recommended for the do-it-your-selfer. There are other places where separation of the wood may cause a buzz, but usually these must be repaired by the factory.

BUZZES IN THE ACTION CHAINS AND ARMS

Buzzes also occur due to wear in the action mechanism, the same type of wear that will cause clicks. Re-riveting is required, which must of course be done at the factory. Sometimes the pedal rods will buzz. If this is the cause, removing them, cleaning and coating with #10 oil may help. (See the section on broken rods.) If two action links have become bent and touch each other, they will cause a buzz. Re-aligning by bending is sometimes required, although sometimes a small strip of felt or adhesive tape can be worked between them. This can be overdone and is not generally recommended.

BUZZES IN THE WIRE STRINGS

A very faint buzz in a wire string may sometimes be the washer behind the stationary nut. Remove it, and make sure the nut is replaced tightly. Use a little oil on the threads of the stationary nut, and proceed with extreme caution. The screw part breaks off easily and a delicate job of removal and replacement may become necessary. Best to leave this to a harp repair man, since a special tool for removing stationary nuts is needed anyway. A poor fit between the wire string and the groove in the nut may cause a buzz or poor tone. Fit a tiny square of pedal felt between the groove and string.

Another common problem in the wire strings is the flutter. It has an unmistakable sound when you have once heard it. Increasing the tension of the back-plate screw is required to prevent the spindle from fluttering in the front plate. The noise will disappear or at least change, if this is the trouble, when you hold the disc lightly in your fingers. Increase the back-plate spring tension by adding steel washers, (not too many, 1 or 2) or on the new type back-plate screw, make a quarter turn clock-wise of the screw and tighten the nut. Check and repeat till corrected. There should be some spring motion in the disc when you push on it. Do not make it completely tight and rigid or it will cause binding and undue wear.

In general, a buzz is caused when two pieces of metal are in contact loosely. The remedy is either to separate them by some soft material or to tighten them so they

117

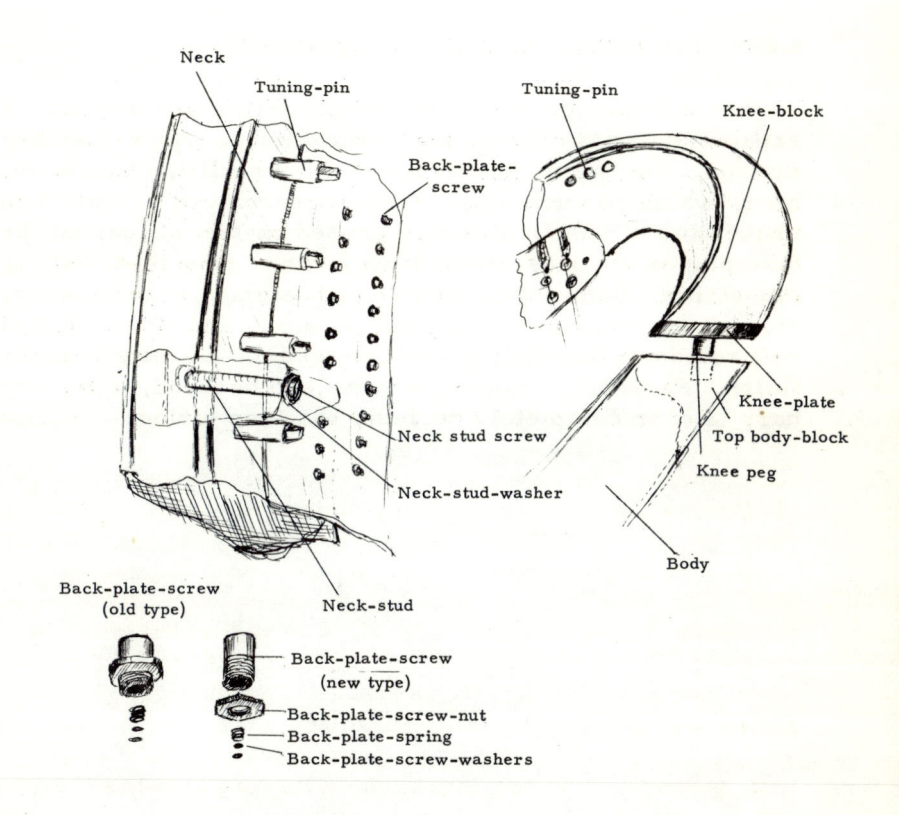

cannot buzz. Wood buzzes are not as loud and are harder to find and repair, but also fortunately they are much more rare.

Rattles will usually be found in the pedal assembly. They are just slower and louder buzzes. Check for metal against metal and correct as above.

KEEP LOOKING, BUT KEEP PLAYING

With all this in mind just keep looking and trying. A repairman could only do the same things. Do remember that on new harps there will be many little buzzes or burrs which go away after it has been played a little and broken in. These are mostly caused by the lacquer on the disc pins which must wear down and be smoothed out by the string. Sometimes you can hasten the process by closing the disc and moving the string in and out so that it will rub down the little groove formed in the new lacquer finish. Persevere, and remember, no husband, wife, nor harp is ever completely perfect, but keep trying.

CHAPTER NINETEEN: BROKEN SPRINGS AND BENT STUDS

Into the life of each harpist sooner or later a broken spring is bound to fall. It has been recorded by one harpist that three springs broke within the space of three days. The mathematical chances against this happening are enormous, unless of course the springs have become rusty. Breakage occurs usually because of metal fatigue. The chances of an old spring breaking are greater by quite a margin. When a new spring breaks it is because of a flaw in the metal, and almost always these flaws will show up in the process of manufacture and cause the spring to break during the winding process; so worry more if your springs are old.

It is easy to tell if you have a broken spring, since the pedal moves smoothly and beautifully, - down -. You will have to pull it up with your toe, however. It probably made quite a noise when it broke, too, if you were there to hear it.

It's a good idea to change all of the springs at the same time because one new spring in with a bunch of old ones will feel much stiffer than the others and cause trouble. The springs will begin to soften and make the action more sluggish after about five years. Change them regularly after such a time.

KEEP A SPARE PAIR

Always keep at least a pair, one right and one left, on hand just for emergency. They will fit nicely into your string bag, or the pocket in the harp trunk. All the springs on each side are the same, that is, a left hand spring will fit the D, C or B, and of course, a right hand spring will fit the E, F, G or A. All styles of Lyon Healy harps and all ages use the same springs, so in ordering, specify right or left and the pedal letter just to be safe.

Some Wurlitzer harps use a slightly different spring, although it is usually possible to make the standard L & H spring fit them. No matter what harp you are fixing, you will find it advisable to fit the spring to the particular pedal by bending it in such a way that in addition to forcing the pedal up, it also forces the pedal more into the notch. This will prevent it slipping out when you want it to stay put.

WATCH OUT FOR THOSE TV CABLES!

The spring studs may sometimes become bent; expecially the long ones that extend far enough down to the floor to be caught if the harp is dragged over something like a TV cable or even a light cord. Proper position of the stud may be determined by checking, with the harp upside down, the movement of the spring. First of all the spring should not touch any wood or metal when the pedal is moved. Second, the winding, with the felt stuffing, should remain nearly motionless in its up and down axis. If it suddenly pops up (this is really down, but remember we have the harp upside down right now) when the pedal is moved into the sharp notch, the stud is too far forward. Carefully bend it back about 1/16th of an inch with a pair of pliers. Be careful! Studs may break; bend them very little at a time. If the pedal springs suddenly flips down as the pedal is moved into sharp, it is too far back; carefully bend it forward. If the spring touches or clicks against the stud or the pedal bar, any pedal bar, bend the stud away as to give the spring clear passage in all its motion.

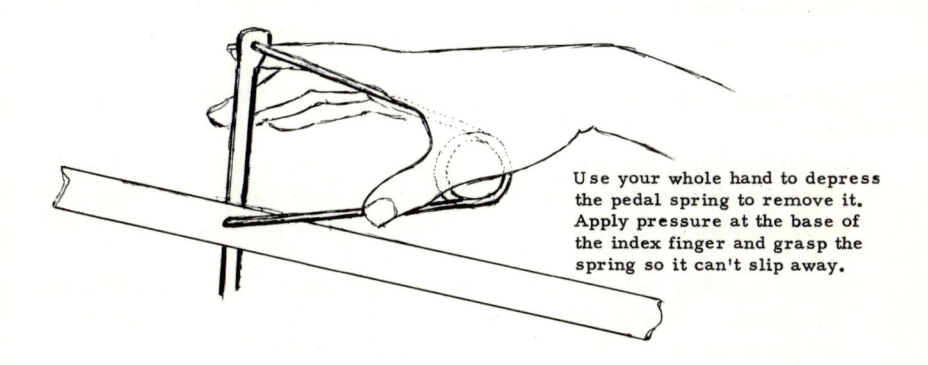

121

Use your whole hand to depress the pedal spring to remove it. Apply pressure at the base of the index finger and grasp the spring so it can't slip away.

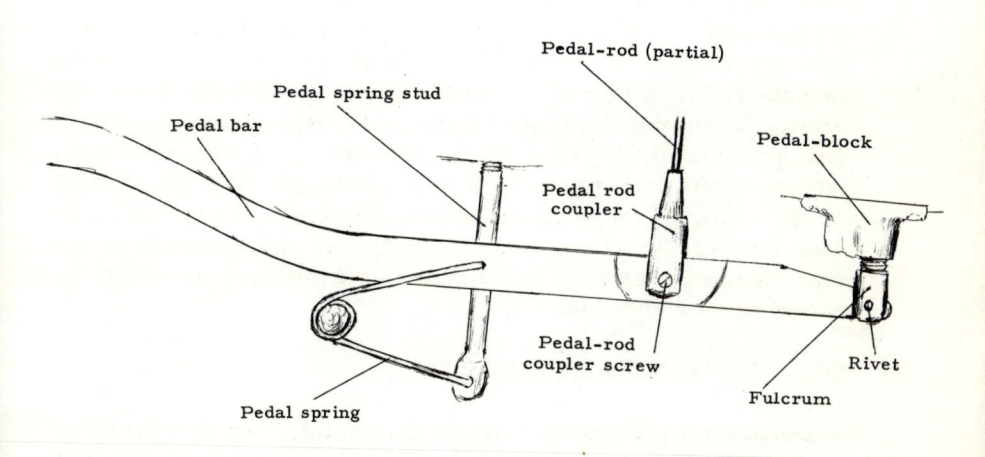

Pedal-rod (partial)
Pedal spring stud
Pedal bar
Pedal rod coupler
Pedal-block
Pedal-rod coupler screw
Rivet
Fulcrum
Pedal spring

In bending, grip the top of the stud with the pliers and force gently. It will bend at the bottom where it is screwed into the wood. This is the weakest spot dur to the threads, so be careful always. Too much back and forth bending will not only cause it to break, but will also spoil the threads in the wood and cause it to be loose. A good rule to follow is: if it works - leave it alone!

WATCH OUT FOR THOSE PEDAL SPRINGS!

Unless you have a strong hand, there is no good method for removing the pedal springs. They are powerful and can be dangerous if they flip out uncontrolled. Always keep your face and eyes away. Do not try to hold the spring down or remove it with just your fingers, because the spring is strong enough to break them. Use the palm of your hand or the base of the index finger and the palm, just under the knuckle. Push with this part of your hand on the upper leg of the spring and depress it slightly; then with your other thumb push it out of the stud. The spring is grooved at this end so that it won't easily slip out of the stud. If you can't get it out this way, use a pair of pliers and gripping the spring near the stud, pull or pry it out. At the same time depress it enough to get the groove out of the stud. If you use the latter approach, keep out of the way in case it slips out of the pliers! Most likely it will stay in the pedal bar, but sometimes they get away and go clear across the room.

OIL THOSE NEW SPRINGS

Before installing the new pedal spring, put a drop of oil on each end; the smooth end which goes into the pedal bar, and the grooved end which will fit into the pedal spring stud. First put the smooth end into the pedal bar, then grasp the winding into the palm of your hand and depress the other leg of the spring, the end with the groove in, under the large knuckle of the first finger as outlined above. Force it down and slip it into the stud. Never try to bend the spring down with only your thumb and a couple of fingers. Always use your whole hand, and still be very careful not to let it get away from you. Keep your eyes and face out of the line of the spring as much as possible.

Make sure that the spring fits all the way into the hole in the stud. You should hear a click as the groove slips into position. Check to make sure the stud is in the correct position, see above, and make sure that the spring does not touch anywhere in its complete motion. Also bend the spring slightly if necessary to make it force the pedal into the notch. This may require removal of the spring a couple of times, and a vise and pair of pliers, but it makes for much safer pedal action.

KEEP SPRING IN YOUR HARP

It is generally wise to keep fairly new springs on the harp for a quick, fast action. If they seem too heavy and you do not feel that you can possibly adjust to them after a little while, they can be softened by bending the legs slightly closer together. Again, a vise and pair of pliers are required, and be certain to get all the springs bent exactly alike. This softening of the springs is really not recommended except for the very young and the very weak, and then since they are so very young or so very weak, someone very strong will have to do it for them; but then this is very much like life.

When replacing a rod, tie the harp securely to a table so that it can't possibly slip.

CHAPTER TWENTY: BROKEN PEDAL RODS

Like broken springs, broken pedal rods can never be predicted. Unlike springs, it is not easy and only rarely advisable to have a spare or two on hand.

Pedal rods are of a different length for each pedal and for each style of harp; also, at different times the same styles had different lengths. To make it even worse, they really have to be fit to the exact length of each harp, since there is a certain amount of variance even between the two harps as they are made in pairs at the factory.

In general the pedal rod is made of .120 inch (120 thousandths of an inch) drill rod, and this material is actually obtainable in most large cities in the United States. It must be cut to the exact length of the old rod, before it was broken, of course. Just fit the broken piece to the long piece and measure the new material against it. Both ends must be threaded with a 4/48 die. Unfortunately, this is not a stock size die, but a good complete machine shop may have one. Try to get them to thread the rod for you, since doing it will take a little skill. Thread about 5/8th inch on one end, which end, incidentally, will be the upper end, going into the column first; and 1 1/4 inches on the other end.

NEW RODS CAN BE ORDERED PRE-CUT FROM THE FACTORY

The simplest way to take care of all the above, if you have time, is to order by phone or telegram from the Lyon Healy harp factory. Specify which rod you need by pedal letter, serial number and style of your harp. The rod will be sent fastened to an appropriate sized stick to prevent its being bent and will usually have a new coupler attached. Be very careful not to bend the rod in the process of handling or it will be useless. Be sure to check the length of your old rod against the new one and get the coupler in the exact position if you can.

The above should answer all questions as to the material required to repair a harp with a broken rod, but how do you know when you have a broken rod? And how do you remove it? And how do you get the new rod in, even after it has been obtained?

EASY PEDAL MOTION - NO ACTION MOTION

If your pedal moves easily up and down, but the action discs do not turn, it is almost certain that the pedal rod is broken. Lay the harp down on a padded table for convenient working height. See illustration. Remove the base and check the defective pedal to see if the rod is broken. Usually, this occurs just above the pedal coupler where the threads make the rod the weakest. When you have located the break and the broken rod, remove as much of the pedal assembly as necessary to get a grip on the long portion of the broken rod. Remove the felt. Grasp it firmly with a strong pair of pliers or "vicegrip" and turn counter-clock-wise. The rod will twist for a quarter or half of a turn before it finally breaks free from the upper coupler and can then be completely unscrewed and withdrawn from the column. Remove the coupler screw and coupler from the pedal bar.

Oil the new rod throughout its length; wipe it clean, but leave a thin film of oil. Use a medium to heavy oil, about #10. Insert the rod into its tube, which will be the only tube without a rod in it. You will need a good flashlight or other good light source to see the tubes. They are made of brass and are soldered together all seven in a row, beginning about ten to twelve inches from the bottom of the column. In the new style 30, the tubes are longer and flared out so that they relieve much of the sidewise strain on the rods and also reduce friction. They will be easier to see, but the process is the same. Insert the new rod into the tube; push it up until it can be seen at the top where the wooden action block was. If you haven't already removed the action block, do it now, and also remove the strip of felt stuffed into the column at the top, just below the action. You will now need some assistance. With the harp resting on its column with the knee block in the air, tie it in this position. Knot a light rope around the leg of the table, take it up on an angle and loop it several times around the neck near the knee block and then extend it down to the opposite table leg and tie it securely. Again, see illustration.

When you can see the tip of the new rod, have your assistant guide it into the upper pedal rod coupler. This will be one of the seven in a row, but the only one with no rod. It will most likely be resting on the wood of the column. Take a small hooked wire and lift it to a position so that it will make contact with the new rod when it is pushed all the way up. Then you will have to lift both the rod and coupler slightly until they are lined up and the rod can be screwed into the coupler. It must be screwed in from the bottom, the same as the old rod was unscrewed, with a good strong pair of pliers. Screw it all the way in and make sure that it is firm.

MATCH THE NEW ROD WITH THE OLD ONE

Now, if you have been careful to check the length of the

new rod with the length of the old rod and to make sure that the couplers are at exactly the same place, your pedal adjustment should be fairly correct. Attach the new coupler and rod to the pedal bar. Replace the base and check for over-movement. Check to make sure it goes easily into sharp. If it does not, take a couple of turns counter-clock-wise with the coupler. If it goes easily into sharp, but the natural disc moves still more when the pedal is moved from natural to sharp, take a turn or two clock-wise with the coupler. Review the section on regulating especially concerning over-motion. Repeat the above two checks until the regulation is satisfactory.

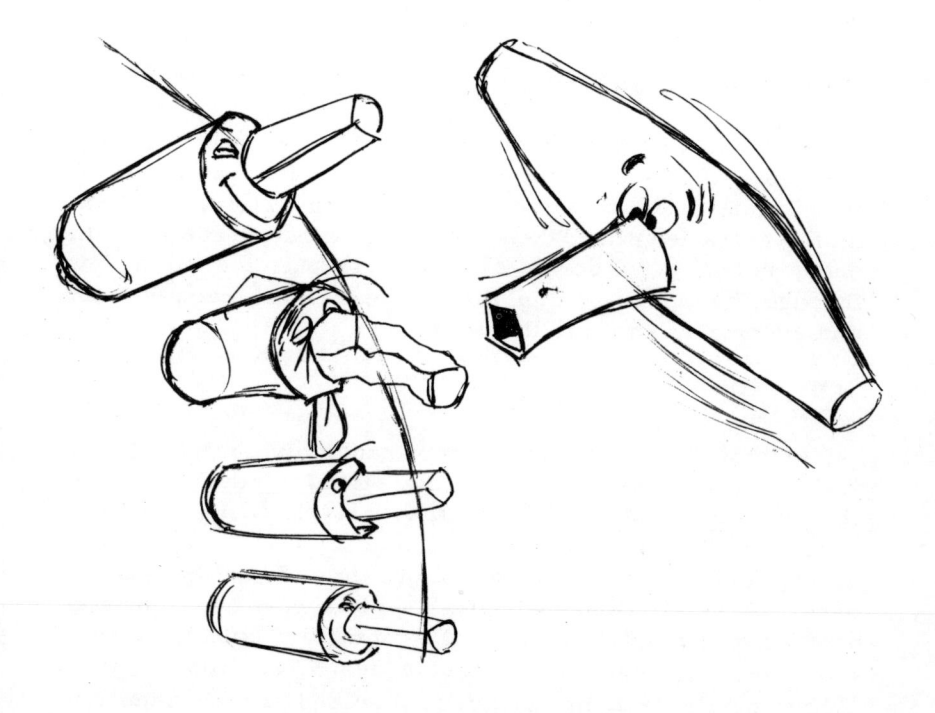

Tuning pins rarely cause trouble unless they are abused.

CHAPTER TWENTY-ONE: TUNING PIN TROUBLES

Tuning pins are rarely a problem, and the few troubles that may occur can be easily avoided by a little regular attention.

Never use a tuning key that is too large and fits loosely on the tuning pins. A drum key or something similar may work for a little while, but will spoil the milled ends of the pins and make costly replacements necessary. Make it a habit to get the tuning key all the way on the pin before you try to tune it. Otherwise you may not only spoil the milling, but break off that end of the pin altogether.

WATCH THAT WINDING

Check the windings of your strings, especially the large ones, and if it has more than three or four windings so that it gets close to the neck, loosen the string and take up the extra length. When the string winding reaches the neck, it acts as a screw or wedge to pull the tuning pin through the neck, making the pin extremely hard to turn and eventually spoiling the neck.

JERKY PINS

For tuning pins that do not turn smoothly, but stick and jerk, remove the string and the pin altogether. Scrape the pin with a coarse file on the scratch filing you will see. This may have become worn quite smooth and should be kept quite deep. Then clean out the hole in the wooden neck. A small fingernail file is often just the right size and taper for this. Scrape it around the hole to remove any loose wood-dust or corrosion deposits. Don't overdo it, but maple is a pretty hard wood and the chances are that you couldn't really enlarge the hole with only a small file. Usually just a turn or two around the hole with the file will do it. Never put chalk nor rosin, nor anything else on the pin nor in the hole! It is always a good idea to clean the pins this way whenever you put on new strings, especially wire ones, since they are not easily removed and replaced.

SLIPPING PINS

If your harp is new, it is probably that the pins will not be perfectly seated at first and may slip slightly. To correct the problem, always push in on the pin as you turn it in tuning. It might be a good idea once in a while to twist the pin back and forth pushing it into the neck at the same time. Do not put rosin or anything else into the tuning pin hole, and do not pound on the pins. You may miss and mar the neck, and the pushing-in-while-twisting treatment is far more effective anyway.

A frozen pedal means a frozen action
and may well chill your heart.

CHAPTER TWENTY-TWO: FROZEN PEDALS

When you discover one day that one of your pedals is a little sluggish in returning to flat and finally refuses to go up at all, you probably have what we in the business call a "frozen pedal," and well may it chill your heart. Usually, it will occur going into flat and more rarely going into the sharp notch.

It is caused by a bit of corrosion, rust or whatever, that comes between one of the little steel rivets that joins the action link to the action arm. A good oil job may even loosen some corrosion that has been lying harmless for years and allow it to move into a position where it can freeze the pedal. This is the reason why a harp should be kept oiled and never allowed to dry out.

Actually, it is not the pedal that is frozen, but the particular chain in the action. There have been theories advanced as to why it occurs most often in flat, and our favorite is that it is of course almost impossible to get at that chain in the action, whereas the sharp chain is easily accessible on the underside of the action. Those chains are the ones you can touch with the hand. When you have confirmed your worst fears, what do you do about it? Keep your fingers crossed! There is a good chance that you can work out the problem yourself. It is worth the try, because if not, the action must be re-riveted at the factory with a cost of several hundred dollars.

A LITTLE OIL IN THE RIGHT SPOT

Turn the harp upside down, resting the body against a wall and tie it there since it will be wise to leave it in this position overnight. Obtain a good penetrating oil such as

"Liquid Wrench." Apply it carefully, one drop on each of the action arms where they join the links of the affected chain. This means you will have to use something like a long hypodermic needle. A piece of an old umbrella stave may work if you file it down to a point. The problem is that you must get the oil on those links that are the hardest to get at. Since the harp is upside down, they are the bottom row, under those action links which you have so often held quiet when looking for that buzz. Just get a good light and get down on your knees and go to it. Do not be intemperate in using too much oil. Don't pour it nor spray it. A little in the right spot is what is needed and then you won't have a big mess to wipe up for the next two months. Getting down on your knees is just the right term too, we think, since several hundred bucks are at stake!

AFTER THE OILING COMES THE WORK

With the oiling done, let the harp remain in the upside down position for about twenty-four hours. Turn it up and try the pedal. Still the same? Don't give up, now the work begins.

The pedal will most likely move up just a little bit from natural so hold it in natural with your foot, but don't lock it in the notch. Now allow your foot to slide off the pedal tip so that the pedal is snapped up by the spring. Even forcing the pedal up by pushing it from underneath will not be as effective as allowing it to snap up since this uses the momentum of the action and keeps the rod from bending so much. This then forces the frozen link to move just slightly and will ultimately work it free.

Keep up this snapping for fifteen minutes at a time or for as long as you can stand it. You may have to work with little evidence of progress for the first day, but do not give up until you have worked it for at least three days. No doubt you will have worn out the rubber pedal cap, but they are cheap compared to a re-rivet job.

Patience is the word, and usually the problem will work out. If yours doesn't, be philosophical about it, your harp probably needed other factory work done, anyway.

Clicks and clacks may mean a major operation.

CHAPTER TWENTY-THREE: CLICKS AND CLACKS

There are cliques and claques in the harp world, but they are more of an asset than the clicks and clacks with which we are concerned in this chapter.

Modern harp playing makes demands on the action of the harp that were unheard of twenty-five years ago. Jazz requires pedalling that makes even the Magic Fire Music look simple; and use is what wears out the action. The sign of wear? Clicks! These are usually a result of a main action which has become worn by the tremendous pressure of the pedal rods and the string tension on the discs.

The holes in the small main action links are often worn completely egg shaped when they are replaced. There is no possible repair except at the factory where the entire main action is usually replaced with a new one; links, arms, and all. Then the new rivets are lapped to the exact size, and presto, no more click. But this, of course, requires taking the entire harp apart and the entire action apart. All the discs and screws, back plate screws and adjustable nuts must be removed. This requires lots of labor, and unfortunately, all must be done by hand.

ALMOST A NEW ACTION

With all this work to be done, the actual re-riveting is only about half the job. It consists of knocking out, carefully, so as not to enlarge the holes, all the old rivets in every link of every chain. All the holes must be reamed out so that they are all perfectly round again, and unfortunately but necessarily, a little larger. Then the new rivets are fitted in, riveted in place and the action reassembled. The plates are usually polished, which, incidentally, is the only way they can be really cleaned, and the discs replated, so that the action comes back looking like new. It is indeed almost as good as new, except that the new larger rivets will wear just slightly faster than the old ones because of their greater size.

CLACKS

As we learned in the section on buzzes, a flutter is caused by too little tension from the back plate screw. A clack is heard when the back plate screw is missing altogether. A clack is also heard when a pedal spring bumps against some part of the pedal assembly. It is simply a large click and is usually easier to locate.

Check first the back plate for missing screws, or possibly a missing spring inside the back plate screw of the offending pedal. Next, check the pedal assembly. You may find on old harps that the base board and sound board have become quite out of line and allow the pedal bar, usually the C, D or B to strike one of the steel stirrups. Not much can be done in this case since it means that the sound board is badly pulled up, and the only permanent remedy is to replace it. If you can find a way to improvise, such as a piece of felt glued to the stirrup or other such measure as ingenuity may show you, --bravo!

Also, check the pedal coupler screws to make sure they are snug and tight. They may cause a slight clack. The spring may also clack due to the way it sets in the groove. A very slight rotation of the spring stud may help, but be sure the rotation does not cause other problems.

BROKEN SCREWS

It may happen that one day you find a screw has broken its head off. Such a pity! It most often happens to the disc screws. Actually, it happens very seldom, but we mean to say that it happens more to the disc screws than to the other kinds. In case you do find such a thing, take it slow, and with a needle see if you can rotate the broken part counter-clock-wise and unscrew it out of the disc and spindle. If you can, you have saved yourself some trouble, but if you can't make it budge, call a good locksmith. They will usually make house calls and are experts at removing broken screws. Replacing the screw may be a little more difficult. Most of these screws have forty-eight threads per inch, but they do vary in size from disc to disc and from harp to harp. A well stocked hardware store should have a screw that will match your broken one; take both pieces along. Of course, the best thing is to obtain a replacement from the Lyon Healy factory, since the screws are all specially made, but sometimes time is of the essence, and for that reason we have made the above suggestions.

CAN'T MAKE THAT OPEN DISC STAY CLOSED?

Another problem that can occur with an action is a "loose arm on the spindle." This means that the brass arm which is connected to the link is not firmly attached to the spindle which turns the disc. This happens only rarely, but when it does, it is usually on the wires or heavy gut strings. You can detect it if a disc is always slightly loose on the string; and no matter how often you close the disc and tighten it, it will soon be open again. In extreme cases, it is possible, actually, to turn the spindle by turning the disc. It will feel like a little rachet as you twist.

140

This problem by the way, is usually caused by uncorrected overmotion in the natural disc. Make sure your pedal rods are correctly regulated!

This repair is difficult and should ordinarily be done by the factory as it may require the removal of the action. If you are in a jam, perhaps you can find a good machinist who will help you. The usual repair is to drill a small hole through the arm and the spindle and insert a small tapered pin into the hole. Make sure it is firm, or use a drip of epoxy to make certain that the pin will not fall out. Such a repair on a sharp spindle is at least accessible, but on the natural row it is best accomplished by removing the action.

CHAPTER TWENTY-FOUR: REMOVING THE ACTION

Removing the action is a big project and should not be undertaken without good cause. Do not try it until you have read all of this volume at least once and understand it well. But if you must, and feel qualified, here's how:

Remove all the strings from the tuning pins, but not necessarily from the sound board. The lowest five or six wires will probably break when taken off and will have to be replaced later. The pedal rods must be disconnected from the upper coupler, but you may leave them inside the tubes and column. Be careful in handling so that they will not be bent at any time. Needless to say, they will also have to be removed from the pedals, but then you have already read the section on broken rods and know how to take them out.

All the stationary nuts must be loosened and removed from the action plate. Keep them in order so that they can be replaced exactly where they were! All the little screws on the adjustable nuts must be loosened but not entirely removed from the action plate. They extend slightly through the front plate and into the wood, which will prevent your removing the action if they have not been unscrewed part way.

KEEP EVERYTHING IN ORDER

Remove the neck stud screws from both the front and back plates. Don't lose any of the felt lined washers under these screws on the back plate. With a flat tipped rod or a large nail with the point filed off, just the size of the hole, carefully drive out the neck studs. Start with the one nearest the crown and once it is out, put a large nail or rod through the hole to hold the action there while you remove the rest of the studs. Are you sure you want to go through with this?

When you get to the neck studs in the treble end of the harp, you will no doubt find that the terrific pressure on the neck and action has bent these studs rather severely, and you may experience great difficulty in getting them out. You will also experience even greater difficulty in getting them back in. To increase the problem, you will also find that the action plates and assembly have bent over a period of years so that returning it to its original position may be extremely difficult. Put another holding pin in the place of the next to last treble stud before you remove the last one. After all the studs are out and all the screws backed out enough to allow clearance, remove your holding pins but hold the action in place with one hand. With both hands hold the underside of the action, slowly pull down the treble end, and it will just clear the sound board by a fraction of an inch as it pivots on the action block. When it is clear, slide down the bass end of the action, and it is free.

ACTION DISASSEMBLY

Further disassembly of the action begins with the complete removal of all the discs, screws and nuts, to be followed by removal of the back plate screws, action block screws on the back plate and the spanner screws on the back plate. This should allow the back plate to be lifted off, exposing the small back plate mounted diagonally in the cut-out of the treble. On newer large harps there will be one more slotted screw in the back plate near the cut-out that must be removed to free the back plate. Remove the holding screws of the diagonal small back plate and remove it. Again, it is to be emphasized that all screws, back plate screws particularly, must be kept in order and returned to their original positions. Needless to emphasize, this is true for the discs and adjustable nuts on the front plate. With both the back plate and the small diagonal back plate removed, the action block screws on the front plate may be removed and the action chains can be lifted off the front plate and out of their spindle holes. Further disassembly will involve removing rivets. To reassemble, simply reverse the above directions.

ONLY FOR MECHANICS ABROAD

The above more or less detailed directions have been included since this little volume is intended to serve as a help and guide for harpists all over the world, many of whom will not have any access to a trained harp repairman, but must rely on a good machinist. Most of these are extremely clever fellows who with the above directions and their own common sense and observation will be able to rescue a fair or unfair harpist from almost any extreme of distress.

Any repairs outlined in this book are, of course, to be undertaken at one's own risk since we cannot guarantee the understanding inferred from our poor command of the language nor of the exact conditions which one may encounter in repairing a harp. We do feel, however, that our little volume may provide invaluable assistance and understanding to the inquiring harpist with problems.

CHAPTER TWENTY-FIVE: SQUEAKS AND KAHOOCHES

Squeaks are nearly always in the pedal assembly. Use a medium heavy oil such as a number ten oil, and put a drop, and a small drop at that, on every point where metal moves against metal, including, the pedal fulcrum, both where it is riveted to the pedal bar and where it is threaded and turns in the pedal block; the pedal coupler, both sides of the bar just to make sure; the pedal spring where it goes into the pedal bar and where it joins the pedal spring stud. Also oil the felt packing stuffed in the spring winding. Do it a drop or two at a time so that it can be absorbed. If this dries out too much it may allow the spring to squeak in the winding. All the above must be done with the harp upside down, and, of course, to each of the seven pedals.

Kahooch is a term invented at the Lyon Healy factory to call a sound in a harp which goes "Kahooch." A most descriptive name, and a most annoying sound. Usually a kahooch is rather loud but will work itself out in two weeks or so simply by using the harp. They are sometimes more faint and may persist for longer.

CHECK THE PEDAL FULCRUM

This kahooch type of sound seems as if it would originate in the pedal rod as it moves in the tube, but this is rarely the case. The rods nearly always remain completely silent, even without much care, for the life of the harp. If you want to be sure, you will have to remove the rod, clean it with oil and replace it, leaving a light coat of oil on it. Most often the kahooch is caused by corrosion in the rivet of the pedal fulcrum. You may find it advisable to disconnect the spring and coupler from the pedal and work oil in the fulcrum by moving the pedal forward and back in a complete arc. This should force the bit of rust or whatever to move to a more silent position. If the troublesome pedal happens to be D, C or B, you must disconnect the E, F, G and A pedals to allow it to swing in its full arc. So oil and work all of them thoroughly while you're at it and you may stave off future kahooches from this spot.

Kahooches may occur in the action also. Oiling and working the action should eliminate the problem. It will not be getting a lot of oil on the action that will solve it, but rather getting just one tiny drop in exactly the right place. With the extremely close tolerances required in manufacturing a harp action, it will take time for even a very light oil to work completely into the moving joint. Try to retain your patience. It will be good practice for some of the conductors you will have to work with.

147

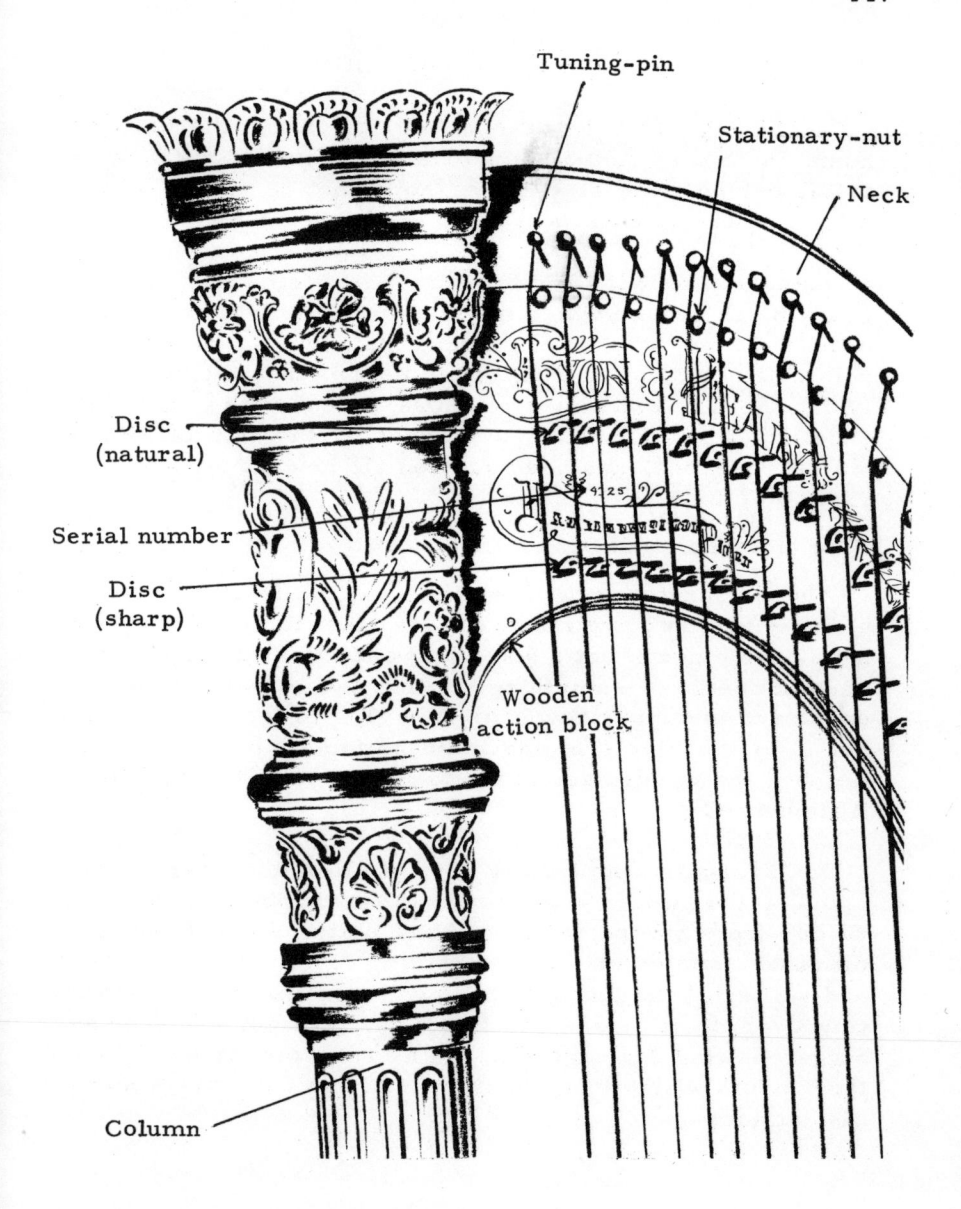

CHAPTER TWENTY-SIX: OIL IT RIGHT!

Sad to say, the traditional way of oiling the harp at home is to take a toothpick or small wire and put a drop of oil behind each disc in the hope that it will ease the motion of the spindle as it turns in the front plate. Fine, but this spot does not take oil. It is lubricated at the time of manufacture with a more or less permanent type of gooey black grease which might only be diluted from your oiling. So we would recommend that you not oil at this point. The exception would be old harps that are obviously dry there. It has been in more recent years that this excellent type of grease, a product by the way of World War II research, has been used on all new harps and re-riveted actions.

GIVE IT THE NEEDLE

Where your action will really need oil is at the brass arms where they are riveted to the steel links. Turn your harp upside down; get a good light and either a long hypodermic needle or something similar and go to it. Both the under and the upper row of links will need the oil. Try to get it to the rivets of the main action up by the crown. Remove the wooden action block so that you can get at it a little better.

Don't forget to put a little drop of oil on the rear of the spindle, too, where it goes into the back plate screw, but do this from the inside of the back plate. Do not put any oil on the outside of the back plate, it won't do any good and will spoil the lacquer finish. Never use more than a tiny drop of oil. Use the finest quality light oil, such as Singer Sewing Machine Oil. The cheaper three in one type of oil will thicken in time and you will have a sluggish action.

A LITTLE OIL IN THE RIGHT SPOT

Use very little oil. Wipe it off after an hour or so. Oil that you can wipe off the action is not in a position to do any lubricating anyway and will only make a mess. This oil will spoil the lacquer if it is left on for too long a time, say a week or two. After oiling your harp, keep a careful check for at least two weeks and wipe away oil drips and runs as they appear. Often there will be an accumulation on the plates where they dip the lowest, at about the third octave. Keep it clean. And for the third time, Don't Use Too Much Oil! Harps are like people, and they shouldn't get well oiled too often. If you oil your harp this thoroughly once a year, that will be plenty.

Now, you have oiled your harp and you've got new problems? It will happen, although pretty rarely, that oiling will free a bit of rust or corrosion that has been out of the way until now and allow it to move into a position where it will squeak, kahooch or even freeze the action. Working the pedal as outlined in the section on the action will ordinarily eliminate the problem within a reasonable time. If you keep your harp oiled, this shouldn't happen, since the problem usually occurs only when a harp is oiled after having been completely dry for years.

There is one last squeak that may drive you out of your mind, in case you ever have to locate it: Does your harp squeak as you pull it back? Do the feet seem to squeak or groan as the harp is rocked slightly from side to side? This is a special problem of the base and will be dealt with in that section.

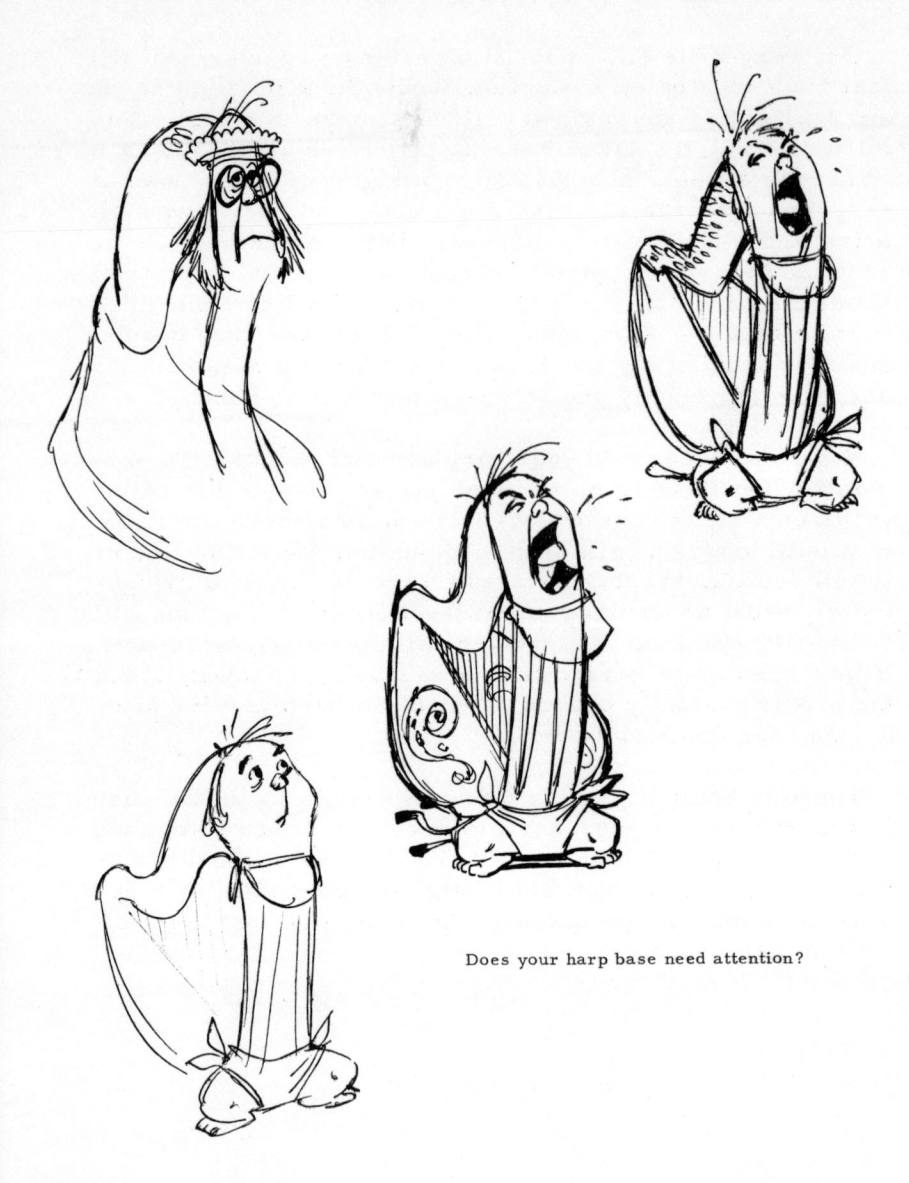

Does your harp base need attention?

CHAPTER TWENTY-SEVEN: THE BASE AND FEET -- SHOES AND INSERTS

How often we equate lower with lesser, and the base as being the least of all. No doubt the base is so taken for granted that we fail to recognize what a complex assembly it is, and how important to the proper functioning of the harp. Being almost altogether of wood, and all of that screwed and glued together, it brooks no further disassembly than simply removing it from the body of the harp. Still, the glue joints may dry out and portions of the base may come loose. This especially if the base has been damp or wet, and then dried out. This happens to two thin flat pieces, one front and one rear, that act as glue blocks reinforcing the joint beneath them. These are the pieces that may come off in case of dampness, etc, but they can easily be glued back on with epoxy. If the glue joint they reinforce is open, it may be a job for the factory, or a good cabinet maker, if you can find one in your area.

The slots may become worn, or the laminations loose. Prompt attention may save you serious repairs later, and it will cut down the wear on your pedal felts. See your good cabinet maker or send the harp to the factory. The wood must have new glue worked into the loose joints and then be clamped. It may even be necessary to add new pieces of wood.

Sometimes the slots will be worn sharp and cut the felts. With sandpaper take off the sharp edge. If the slot becomes polished by the felt, it may be so slick that the pedal doesn't stay in the notch. A little course sandpaper will roughen it slightly. If you have a lot of trouble with the pedal staying in the notch, check the section on broken springs. It may be that your springs need bending so that they force the pedal more into the notch. Above all do not overdo any sandpapering since wood once removed cannot be replaced.

SQUEAK IN THE BASE

If you have the famous squeak in the base that comes when the harp is rocked or pulled back, the chances are that you will find it in the base bolt bushing where it is too loose in the wood. Many harpists exercise a little too much vigor when tightening these base bolts. They should be made firm, but no more than firm. Repeatedly forcing them too tight will pull the base bolt bushing loose from the wood, and this is where you will usually find the squeak.

Remove the bushing by unscrewing it counter-clockwise. The threads in the wood will likely be a mess; clean them out and glue the brass base bolt bushing back in with clear epoxy. Always use the epoxy that dries clear. The white stuff makes a horrible mess; and be sure to clean up all the excess glue immediately with a paper towel which you can throw away. With the epoxy glue, coat the hole in the wood from which you have just removed the bushing. Coat the base-bolt with cold-cream and screw it into the brass bushing. This is to keep the glue from sticking the base-bolt to the bushing. Now insert the bushing, with the bolt still in it, back into the glue coated hole; screw it or force it all the way down so that it is flush with the surface of the base board and even with the wood around its edge.

Unscrew the base bolt. Repeat the process for the other bushings if they are at all loose, and then put the base back on. Put in the base bolts and screw them in part way, but do not tighten them, since we do not want to pull the bushings out again. After the glue has dried, about twenty-four hours, the bolts may be tightened, but remember from now on, only firm, not forced.

On older harps when the board is pulled up, you may see an open space between the base and the body of the harp on the sides just behind the base board, which will likely be touching the base at that point. The body will be in contact with the base only toward the back leaving an open space toward the front. Do not try to close this, because you need a new sound board.

OTHER PLACES TO CHECK

Fixing the base bolt bushings will most often take care of the squeak, but it may also come from a loose glue joint in the rear feet, or perhaps in some of the other joints of the base where the glue may have failed. It will probably not be found between the base and the body. There is felt here which will prevent squeaking; however, it could be from one of the little base pins if it has become corroded and also if the base is loose against the body. Graphite may be applied sparingly. If your base has loose joints, it must be fixed sooner or later, so don't put graphite anywhere that must ultimately be reglued. It will prevent the glue from holding.

As we have already mentioned, the front and rear shoes of the harp are great sources of buzzes and rattles. Keep these screws as tight as possible. If they do become loose in the wood, the proper repair is to fill the old screw hole with a round stick or dowel of just the right size and glue it in. Then drill a smaller hole in the dowel the right size for the screw. Metal will always cause wood to rot, and such unions must be constantly checked and repaired, especially in the case of the shoes which have great strain and are removed from time to time.

Replace your harp shoes too soon rather than too late. They are tempered in such a way that only the surface is hard. The metal beneath this "case hardening" is comparatively soft and will wear away fast once the hard surface is gone. This leaves a sharp edge if it wears all the way through and can cut up a floor or rug badly.

SLIPPERY FLOORS

Inserts in the rear feet are designed to keep the harp from slipping, which they will do if the floor is not polished nor waxed. However, the hard rubber required for durability also prevents them from being completely skid proof. A small rubber mat about two or three feet long is great to have in your trunk for an emergency on a slick marble floor.

Change the inserts as they are worn. They can sometimes be reversed to advantage if you have a slick stage and no spares. These are among the other little items which you should keep on hand, since they are small and inexpensive.

A broken neck is easily diagnosed.

CHAPTER TWENTY-EIGHT:
NECKS - TWISTED AND BROKEN

A harp with a broken neck is one of the easiest problems to diagnose. There is simply no question. There it is, broken!

Usually, a break will occur in a line running between one of the neck stud screws and tuning pin, and nearly always in the first octave. There is no repair except to send it to the factory for a new neck. For the benefit of persons who simply cannot send it to the factory, such as our friends in Tanganika or Australia, we will outline what a neck is, so that a competent draftsman may manage to make a replacement.

FOR CRAFTSMEN ONLY

The neck material is a thirteen ply laminated die block, such as are used in foundry pattern making. It must be of the finest rock hard maple, with no interior nor exterior knots, or of equivalent material. The finished thickness, lacquer and veneers included, must be exactly one and one-half inches with .005 inch tolerance. Make a pattern from the old neck and also use the action as a guide in case of warpage from the original form, and of course the correct positioning of the broken portion. The knee block must be extremely well glued and then shaped to the original pattern.

The dimensions are particularly critical in the extreme treble, and the tolerance for correct positioning of the action is about 1/32nd of an inch. It may be possible to use shims between the knee block and the body to make corrections. The original neck will be glued to the column and has one long screw vertically into the column and usually two more screws diagonally from the sides of the column into the neck. All of the screws are covered by doweling. Good luck!

THOSE CRACKS PROBABLY DON'T MATTER

Cracks in the neck are frightening to most harpists, and most often they are of little or no consequence. They are usually only in the veneer and will, in this case, tend to follow its grain. They may show up near the tuning pins in the base, but other than a rather unhappy appearance, they are nothing to worry about. A crack in the kneeblock, near where it is curved and tapered into the flat part of the neck is all too common. This occurs because of the unusual shape of the wood at this point, which swells and shrinks unevenly due to its varying thickness thus causing cracks. Generally, they do not affect the strength of the neck at this point, and so should not cause undue concern about breakage. Occasionally, a more complete separation will occur between the neck and kneeblock. This is caused by glue failure and can be repaired by cleaning out the old glue with a very thin blade, and working in new glue. Clamping is the problem; use your ingenuity, but try to avoid leaving press marks in the wood.

A crack that runs across the grain of the veneer in the first octave and from a stud screw to a tuning pin should however be watched carefully. With a flashlight, and perhaps a small mirror, you may be able to see the underside of the neck enough to determine if the crack extends across one or more of the layers of lamination. If it does, you may expect trouble, but then harps being the personalities they are, it may go for years and never even happen.

TWISTED NECKS

The most common neck trouble is with old harps when the neck has become twisted so far that the strings do not make good contact with the discs. Sighting down the neck and comparing it with the column is the time honored procedure in determining how far a neck has twisted, but it is usually most misleading. There is a quick and accurate way to tell exactly how far a neck has twisted. The harp must of course be fully strung and more or less up to pitch. Check the fourth octave F and the fifth octave E and the other strings nearby. Do the strings make contact with the disc pins when it is closed in sharp? If they are barely caught by the tips of the disc pins, the neck is badly twisted and should be replaced. Often they will slip out of the grip of the disc if the string is played loudly, or they may be entirely out of reach of the disc.

The wire strings have a washer under the stationary nut. You can see it if it is still there by the knurled or serrated edge between the front plate and the stationary nut. These are put on new harps with the expectation that they will be removed after two or three years to allow the bass strings to come closer in to the neck. They are put there in the first place to keep these large strings from buzzing against the disc screws while the harp is new.

ALL NECKS TWIST

The necks of all new harps will twist slightly in the first couple of years, and then remain fairly constant for the life of the harp. The washers are a means of allowing for this. They should be removed no later than five years after the harp was made as they will ease slightly the torque tension the strings exert on the neck. There is really no way to straighten a badly twisted neck, and replacement is necessary. As sound-boards are replaced mostly because they are pulled up too far to regulate, most necks are replaced because they are twisted too far to allow the discs to make good contact with the strings.

A makeshift repair often seen is to file a new groove for the string in the nut a little closer in to the front plate. This does bring the string in close enough for the disc to make contact, but it is now much closer to the disc screw in the upper row and may buzz against it. A similar but tidier repair is to have a machinist cut the nuts a little shorter. This leaves you with the same problem as above. Both these repairs will make it necessary to replace all such filed parts when the neck is finally replaced, so the extra expense would cancel out any saving from such a repair.

There is a trick that may sometimes work if the neck is not too bad. Back off the disc a couple of turns, clockwise. This will give you another fraction of an inch and may make the difference in the disc gripping the string. It is quick and easy and does no damage to the mechanism. It is not possible to obtain new discs with extra long pins as a regularly stocked item; however, certain style harps at certain periods had a little different design for their discs and some of these were with longer pins. The junk boxes at the factory or harp studios sometimes have such pins, if they can be found; so, if you are nearby, it won't hurt to inquire.

CHAPTER TWENTY-NINE: SOUND-BOARDS -- CHECKS, CRACKS, BREAKS OR JUST PULLED UP

Sound-boards have always been made of spruce, but recently it was discovered that a harder wood made for a more resonant tone, and a number of harps were made with sugar maple boards. These were veneered in the usual way with the very thin covering of spruce that the old boards had, and so are indiscernible from the regular boards except by looking inside the body of the harp. The boards were successful and had a good brilliant tone, but have been temporarily discontinued as of this writing because of climatic control problems at the factory. No doubt these problems will be licked and such boards may again become available. They have, as mentioned, an excellent tone, but do take longer to break in.

"Breaking in" is a mysterious process that seems much akin to black magic. Actually, it is a logical and natural process that can be explained.

1600 POUNDS

Each string on the harp is pulling up on the sound-board with an average tension of at least 35 pounds. This means that you would have to hang a 35 pound weight from the string in order to bring it up to pitch, or to equal the tension applied by the tuning pin. With 46 or 47 strings on your harp, this then makes the total applied string tension about 1600 to 1650 pounds. It is no wonder that the necks twist and the boards pull up.

In the process of breaking in, this tension must obtain some degree of balance. The board will pull up quite rapidly for the first few days after it is strung up. It does not pull really very far, but theoretically at least, each vibration of a string pulls the board up a tiny fraction and then the elasticity of the board returns it exactly to its original position making the complete vibration cycle period. When the board is new and still adjusting to the pull of the strings, it yields a little to each vibration; the new board is not perfectly elastic and so does not quite return to its original level. Gradually, the pull down of the board will exactly equal the pull up of the strings; the stresses are balanced and this part of the breaking in process is more or less complete. A similar adjustment of stress balance must obtain in the twisting of the neck, although this has a less significant effect on the tone of the harp.

KEEP A NEW HARP WELL TUNED

Concurrent with this, other processes less obvious are also going on. These involve the plasticity of the wood, the moisture content of the wood, and that mysterious process known as aging. All of this together seems to be affected by the playing of the instrument, and even by the quality of tone produced by the player! It would seem that there occurs some form of alignment of the small wood fibres in their more liquid and pliable surrounding materials. This allows for symmetrical or regular concentration of material and causes a greater response to that particular type of tone that caused such an alignment in the breaking in process. In other words, a harp will gradually tend to reinforce the type and quality of tone that is played on it.

BREAK IN A HARP BY PLAYING
WITH THE BEST POSSIBLE TONE

This effect is noted on all string instruments. Violins

and cellos particularly seem to take on the type of tone of the person who plays them, and the new owner of even a very old fiddle must break it in to his own tone quality!

It is probable that as the wood ages and loses more of its moisture content it also loses its plasticity or ability to change; thus, the quality of tone would become more permanent.

CLIMATIC PROBLEMS

In our American climate, wood generally dries to about an eight percent moisture content and is kept more or less stable at this figure by the moisture content of the air. In European products wood must be dried to about fourteen percent where it will remain more or less stable. This accounts for some of the problems encountered in bringing European instruments or even furniture to this country where the wood will gradually dry to our eight percent, drying out the glue joints and causing them to fail and open up.

Extreme variations will be encountered in certain areas such as proximity to a large body of water or desert. Moisture on a humid day may cause the board to swell and will cause the strings, even wires and nylons to go flat. Gut strings will stretch more in high humidity and add to the problem. This swelling and shrinking of the board due to humidity causes an all too common but almost unavoidable problem: checking.

SOUND-BOARD CHECKS

A check is a small hair line crack occuring in the thin veneer covering the sound-board proper. This veneer has the grain running vertically and its primary purpose is

A vertical crack in the sound-board may be only a check and nothing to worry about.

better appearance. It does seem to bind the board together, however, and make for a more enen tone throughout the harp. The veneer has been put on nearly all harps made within the last fifty years, and earlier harps do not have it unless they have had new sound-boards put on.

This crack in the veneer in no way affects its strength or ability to hold the board together. It is simply unsightly and has no effect on the tone or structural strength of the harp. There is no repair short of reveneering, and no way to prevent them short of keeping the harp in a constant temperature and humidity controlled environment. They are not covered by the guarantee. Forget them.

PULLED UP?

The big problem with sound-boards is that they pull up. There is no predicting how long a board will last. Some have gone more than sixty years, and others have been replaced after twelve years. The amount of moving and travel a harp undergoes seems to have an effect on the life of a board, even though it is moved carefully. If a harp is moved a lot and played a lot, it simply wears out faster. This is the only philosophical way to look at it. When a sound-board is pulled up too far, it is virtually impossible to do a good regulating job on it, and, therefore, it must be replaced.

Boards rarely break entirely and almost as rarely pull loose from the body. When this happens it is usually on harps with extended boards made more than forty years ago. Since that time the factory has added three brass wing bolts which can be seen only from the under side of the wing. These add the necessary strength to this part of the board and have been most effective in preventing this type of pull up.

BROKEN BOARDS

When a board does break, it is usually in a straight vertical line extending through the third, fourth and fifth octaves right next to the center strip. Such a line may only be the veneer severely cracked and pulling loose from the board, but even this may be a precursor to a complete break in the board at this point. There is no repair for a broken board and complete replacement is necessary. Again this is a factory job, but we will for the benefit of our really far out harpists try to give enough details that a competent craftsman in Madagascar, for instance, might be able to help them out.

REMOVE THE OLD BOARD FOR A PATTERN

The old board on a harp can be removed carefully and used for a pattern. Plane or pry off the glue strips at the edge of the board. Remove the screws underneath and then pry the board free all around. Dowel the old screw holes with hardwood pegs and glue. Plane or sand it level, but do not remove any more wood than absolutely necessary. The final outside dimensions are critical.

Sound-boards are traditionally made of spruce, and due to the manufacturing problems in the use of hard woods, stick to it. Select the finest obtainable Sitka spruce with perfectly straight grain. Cut it into three inch widths, and cut them into lengths so that laid edge to edge they will cover the board area and allow for waste. Check the vertical grain of the wood and make sure it runs approximately parallel to the direction the strings will take on the reassembled harp. The edges of the three inch pieces should be perfectly jointed and then glued together. The factory uses hot glue of the highest quality.

Cut the assembly to the approximate outline of the finished board, but still allow one-half inch or so for waste. Plane the upper surface flat and apply 16th of an inch veneers matched face to face with the grain running vertically. Plane the back of the board so that it is tapered from one-half inch at the base to about 1/8th inch at the treble. Sanding should leave the finished dimension around 3/32nds at the treble. You may be able to salvage the old bridge and center strip, but if not, at least use them as patterns to make new ones.

Make and install new sound-board ribs matching the old ones. Fit the board to the body, making certain of a tight fit between the bottom body frame and the bottom of the bridge. Shim with hard wood if necessary. The board is then glued all around the edges and screwed with small screws about every three-fourths of an inch. Trim the waste off to the exact edge of the body, and reveneer the sides. Cover the screws with a new glue strip as originally, and fit in corner strips to cover the joints.

Eyelets are used all the way to the top on all new harps. They are cut on a lathe from nylon rod. The buttons in the base are plain nylon rod of the correct dimension. These latter must be grooved for the wire strings after the harp is completed. The hook and stirrups can be removed from the old board and fitted to the new work.

Many harpists cling to an old pulled up board on a harp long after it should have been changed. The regulation is not the only thing that suffers when the board is too high.

The shortened strings then lack tension, and consequently, many of the upper partials which give the tone richness and carrying power are lost. The tone sounds fat and tubby on these old harps and is misleading since it sounds big right under the ear. Actually, a rich brilliant tone on a harp will often sound rather disagreeable and harsh if you are too close to the instrument. Space and air softens this and the overtones are actually heard as reinforcing the fundamental adding to its brilliance and beauty.

NEW BOARD PLUS OLD HARP
EQUALS GREAT INSTRUMENT

A new board on an old harp will often take the best from both situations. The old parts of the harp impart the beauty of their aging, and the new board, once it is broken in, lends its strength and beauty with excellent results. So do not fear to replace that old board with the washboard ripples. These, by the way, show that the glue all around the edge of the board is dried out and the board is being held only by the screws. The craftsmanship at the factory is still in the old pride-of-hand-work tradition, and it is aided by some up to date machinery which gives greater accuracy; for example, in the sound-board taper. Your old harp may turn out to be an even greater harp than you've always thought, and you might even get that regulation in the first and second octaves fixed!

CHAPTER THIRTY: THE BODY AND THE BASE-BOARD STIRRUPS AND HOOKS

The body is made very much like a small canoe at first. The frame inside is made and the two side panels are then fitted and glued on. The metal ribs are fitted in to add strength and stability. Style 30s are made a little differently since the strength comes from the panels themselves rather than the frame, and it uses all wood construction with no metal ribs which affect the tone. The flat panels also serve as additional sounding boards since they will vibrate much better than curved plywood.

The craftsman who builds the harp takes the roughly assembled body and adds the wings, back panel, top and bottom body blocks and sound-board, also doing all the related steps and work involved.

BODY BLOCKS

The style 30 needs no body blocks, so if you have a 30 you can forget about them. On the old style body, these blocks serve to hold the side panels together at the top and at the bottom. Most old harps do have at least a slight opening between these blocks and the panels. If the opening is only slight, and is not spreading, it may well stay that way for years; but when the board is replaced, they should be repaired. Only in severe cases, where the side panel shows signs of buckling and is clearly pulled loose from the body block inside, will immediate repair be needed.

TAKE CARE OF THE FINISH

Some polishes, cosmetics and sometimes just plain

perspiration and wear will take off all the lacquer finish on the sides of the body. This will show up as a dark spot and may be nothing to worry about. But, it is possible then for an excess of moisture to get at the wood with the finish gone and cause a blistering effect with the layers of wood coming apart. Repair is difficult even at the factory, and a new body may be required. Expensive? Yes! Take care of these spots, either by yourself or have a touch-up man from a good furniture store fix it.

PRESSURE

The base-board is the focal point for much of the 1600 pounds of pressure exerted by the strings. It must be strong. Support is gained by the steel stirrups which fasten it to the sound-board. There are also a couple of big screws from the hole in the base-board into the sound board. Still, the base-board will sometimes crack and show signs of going down under the terrific pressure. This may call for immediate action.

If it is not possible to ship it to the factory, disassemble the harp and remove the base-board from the body by removing the stirrup screws and the two screws in the column hole that connect it to the body. It may be possible to repair the base-board if there is room to reinforce it underneath with steel straps. Usually, however, it is about as easy to have a new one made. A good cabinet maker should have little difficulty in duplicating it. The column block, that wooden ring on the base-board that the column fits in to, is glued and often screwed on. If it can be removed and salvaged, so much the better; if not, a new one will have to be made. This calls for some tricky turning on a lathe to make it thinner at the front. The style 11 does not have a separate column block, since it is carved as an integral part of the base-board. It may be easiest for your cabinet maker to do it this way, especially if he has a duplicating carving machine.

PUT EVERYTHING BACK LIKE IT WAS

Make some sort of pattern so that you can place the old hardware exactly in its correct position on the new baseboard. The position of every screw should be carefully marked since each is critical. The base bolt bushing should be screwed into threaded holes, but since wood threaders of this size are rare, make a hole with a snug fit, and glue it in with clear epoxy. About the finish, a good cabinet shop can do that, too, if it is natural. If it must be gold leafed, try a picture frame gilder.

The harp today is moving ahead.

CHAPTER THIRTY-ONE: COLUMNS AND CROWNS

The column is also a complex assembly. It is made up of twenty-one pieces of wood and is hollow inside. The two main center pieces are grooved before gluing so that there is a hollow shaft inside to accomodate the pedal rod tubes, and, of course, the rods themselves. After it is all glued together, it is turned on a lathe to the rough shape that it will finally be; then it is rough carved on a machine to the outlines of the design pattern and returned for fine turning on the lathe. Finally, it is given to the hand carver for his artistry. The style 30 column is made much the same except that it is not turned on a lathe, but carved to the five sided shape on a machine and then finished to a perfect surface by hand.

Columns rarely give trouble, but have been known to come apart at some of the glue joints. If this type of opening becomes large enough to slip a piece of paper in to, you had better ship the harp off for repair. The Salzedo model, long since discontinued due to their complexity and slight demand, had after thirty years or so shown an inherent weakness in the column where the neck is inserted. The structure is not thick and strong near the neck, and its tapered plane surfaces seem to cause the wood to warp away from the neck. Repair is not too difficult and could be attempted by first cleaning out carefully all the old glue in the open joints. With benzine remove all possible grease and dust. Apply clear epoxy and make sure it covers all the surfaces to be joined. Then with several wooden clamps force the open joint, or joints, closed. This may take some muscle, but should be possible. Place the clamps carefully so that they are exactly flat on the wood surfaces or you will mar the wood. Wipe off all excess glue immediately. On all gluing you should see "squeeze-out" or the excess of glue that comes out from between the two pieces when pressure is applied. This shows that you do have enough glue. But at least in this case where it is coming out on to a finished surface, make sure you wipe it off immediately, or you will have an awful mess. A repair similar to this could be attempted on other column openings. Special care must be taken in clamping or press marks will show in the wood.

BROKEN CROWNS

A crown is still a most important item to many harpists, although originally it was put on the harp to hide an unsightly and otherwise indisguisable joint where the neck and column meet. The metal crowns are broken occasionally, but can be replaced by ordering by style and serial number from the factory. The same with wooden crowns. Exceptions may be metal crowns for the smaller gilded harps, since these have not been made for many years, and the stock of spare crowns for them has dwindled.

CHAPTER THIRTY-TWO: BENCHES AND STANDS

A special music stand to match your harp is a charming luxury. It will fit into the trunk and add much to the appearance of your harp, whereas the less expensive metal stand may not. They are also heavy enough to be stable under a load of music. If the cost is added to the price of your new harp, it will scarcely be felt and will, with care, last as long as the harp.

That "with care" is what we now discuss. The stand is easily disassembled, by taking out the thumb screw and removing the desk. If you replace the thumb screw in its place, it won't get lost; but, do not tighten it.

The metal on the top of the brass shaft is a very weak white metal and will break easily. Tightening the thumb screw squeezes the two sides together and they will break before you know it. The shaft with this piece attached must be ordered from the factory, and the cost is about ten dollars.

The wooden shaft is removed by unscrewing the nut that holds it to the base of the stand. Replace the nut so that it won't be lost. And do feel free to make this one as tight as you want; you can't break anything, and you are the one who has to unscrew it again.

The harp bench is no luxury; it is a real necessity. A harpist can adjust to almost any playing height for the harp, as long as it is always the same. Taking chances on chairs and rolled covers is never good. Get a bench. They come about 19 3/4 inches in height, but can have, the legs shortened to make them lower if desired. This is usually done by the purchaser. The legs screw into the upper part of the bench because there are some nuts hidden under the corner glue blocks which coincide with the holes for the leg bolts. If these nuts wear away enough wood, they may turn around with the bolt when you try to screw it in, and you can never get them tight. Call on your cabinet maker friend. Remove the glue blocks; check the position of the nut and either glue it or shim it with wood so that it can't rotate, still making sure that it lines up with the hole. Replace the glue block and you're in business again.

It is recommended that both the bench and the stand be included in the price of a harp when purchased since the extra hundred dollars or so will not add much to the pain of the moment, and the bench and stand will add much to the joy and comfort not to mention ability of the harpist.

Harpists tend to seek each other out!

CHAPTER THIRTY-THREE: OF WOOD AND GLUE

We have bandied the word 'wood' about a good deal, but just what is it? Wood is a relatively light fibrous material with a specific gravity averaging about .65. There are thousands of different kinds, each with different properties. In the harp we are concerned primarily with two properties in which wood excells all other material. Strength and lightness are immediately obvious since the harp must be light enough for the player to handle, and yet strong enough to stand years of tremendous tensions and pressures.

Rock hard maple, native to America, fills this role admirably and is used extensively in the structural parts of the harp. Some other woods are used for special construction problems: poplar for some glue blocks; bass wood for other forms that must not warp; beech and birch for the bridge and center strips. Rosewood, walnut, satinwood, korina, mahogany and other ornamental woods have been used in the side strips and veneers.

WOODEN AMPLIFIER

The second property of wood in which we have great interest is its ability to act as an amplifier for sound. The same high ratio of strength to lightness is no doubt the reason for wood's excelling in this respect also. Spruce has been traditionally used in pianos, harpsichords, violins and all the string family.

Recent research has shown that a hard wood actually offers more reasonance than spruce and with its high ratio of strength to lightness means that a hard wood sound board could be made light enough to offer the best in a beautiful brilliant tone, and yet be strong enough to stand the years of tension without ever pulling up.

MAPLE SOUND-BOARD ON THE VIOLIN

A little reflection will bring to mind that the violin family has always used a maple or similar hard wood in the back. This being connected to the bridge by the sound post means that it would probably be the primary sounding board and would act as a greater amplifier of the sound than the spruce breast! So maybe this research didn't discover anything so new after all.

SCREWS AND NAILS

Cabinet makers and craftsmen in wood have known for thousands of years that if two pieces of wood are joined by a piece of metal, such as a nail or a screw, they will sooner or later come loose. The unequal reactions to temperature and humidity of the two materials would naturally cause a working loose. Also, metal has a tendency to corrode under the moisture in wood, which in turn has a deleterious effect on the wood and hastens the whole loosening process.

The Mormon pioneers in Salt Lake City, Utah built their Tabernacle entirely of wood, and this enormous structure was built without any nails or screws! This all wood construction may be partially responsible for the famous sound that the building has. It was not entirely because they had no nails that they were not used in the building. The large timbers are put together with large pegs, more than three inches in diameter. These were used as bolts with a wedge in each end making for a rigidity of construction that seems not one bit loosened after a hundred years.

This applies to the harp in that all of its pieces are put together with glue. Until very recently the best glue known was hot gelatin glue. Indeed the author is acquainted with workers at the factory who have used the very same glue powder that they mix with water in their glue pots to make a tasty gelatin dessert for their lunch! The glue as it comes to the factory actually bears a pure food and drug label. Recent discoveries in the field of adhesives add to the potential of improving harps. Various types of waterproof glues have taken over where the old water soluble glue could be improved.

Screws are, to be sure, not indispensable on the harp. Where the various assemblies must be taken apart from time to time they are just screwed, but where the greatest possible strength must be obtained, both glue and screws are used. The most evident spot such as this is the sound-board which is both glued and screwed all the way around. In old harps where the glue has dried out, and the board is a little loose, the washboard effect can be felt near the edges. The screws will go on holding very well sometimes for years, but it usually means that the board has been allowed to slip side ways toward the strings and will be quite high. If you are considering a second hand harp, watch for this, and if you find it, plan on replacing the board in about five to ten years.

Until about 1959, all the necks made at the factory were seven-ply laminations put together with a waterproof glue. Now, the neck material is made up at a wood mill, and the pieces are not glued, but bonded. This implies much greater pressure and heat in the process of assembly so that there is virtually no filler space of binding material, such as glue, between the pieces, and they are almost welded into one. Such a neck promises much greater life and freedom from twist.

CHAPTER THIRTY-FOUR: THE FINISH - PRESERVING AND REPAIRING

Your harp is finished with about six coats of the highest quality lacquer and rubbed down between each coat. Lacquer is impervious to most liquids, but constant or repeated applications of certain things may soften it. Detergents will soften lacquer. Never use them on your harp. For this same reason avoid self polishing waxes. The best thing to clean your harp with is a slightly damp cloth and perhaps a little flax or vegetable oil soap. A cream oil polish may help to add luster, but make sure from the supplier that it will not harm lacquer. Still, wipe it off thoroughly after applying.

CLEANING THE ACTION PLATE MEANS TROUBLE

The action plates cannot really be cleaned except be removing the action and disassembling it completely. The exception to this would be a person with enough determination to try hard enough. The lacquer will have to be removed from the plates, the brass cleaned, and then a new finish put on. And all this must be done without damaging the discs or strings nor diluting the spindle grease! But it has been done and it didn't look too bad when it was finished.

CLEAN AWAY LINT AND OIL

Routine cleaning of the action, however, is a must. Lint will accumulate from the cover, and it should be brushed away often. A small stiff brush and a pipe cleaner will serve in good stead. Always wipe away oil stains as soon as they appear.

GOLD LEAF

Even the gold leaf is covered by a coat of lacquer, so treat it the same as the rest of the harp. In general, it is not a good idea to try to touch up a gold column. What is left of the original finish is almost always better than what repairs can be done to it. A factory regilding job is exceedingly expensive, $1,000, or so. A touch-up job there is not very much less.

GOLD PAINT

Never use gold paint on a harp! It turns a greenish brown within a few months and will look worse than it ever could have before. If you have such a job on your harp already, you can remove the brown paint by carefully and gently going over it with a soft cloth dampened in lacquer thinner. Even a gold column that has become dull (not worn) can be brightened this way. Remember that you must apply a new coat of clear lacquer after you have removed the dull paint, or else the gold leaf itself will wipe away. The lacquer thinner will not remove the gold, but persistent rubbing with the cloth will! Just get the brown paint off and quit while you're still ahead.

As mentioned before, a picture frame maker often has a gilder who can put on gold leaf. It has been our experience that these men, though they have years of experience, do not do the same type of gilding as is done on your harp. This lost art is practiced at this time by only one man at the factory who learned it from the man before him, who learned it from . . ., etc. It is not just a secret, it is a complex skill, even to tasting or feeling the glue and clay to make sure they are just right for the temperature and humidity of that particular day!

A good cover will provide some protection from nicks
and scratches but none from cold and humidity.

NICKS AND SCRATCHES

Little nicks and scratches incurred in the normal life of a harp can be repaired by a "touch-up" man, such as a skilled gentleman ordinarily employed by fine furniture or piano stores who travels for them to touch up little nicks and scratches incurred in the normal delivering of their products. Get in touch with the store and find out who the man is. Style 30s especially with their darker finishes respond very well to such repair; ten or fifteen dollars can make one of these look just like new.

Some harpists militantly maintain that
they have the world's greatest harp!

CHAPTER THIRTY-FIVE: ANTIQUE HARPS

WHAT IS AN ANTIQUE?

Not many pedal harps around today can really be classed as "Antiques" since that definition by law requires an age of at least 150 years in most places. Still, we will find in odd shops and attics, occasionally, an old harp that certainly looks the part. Some of the owners are unscrupulous enough, or ignorant enough, to sell these for rather exorbitant prices.

The oldest harp we have had the pleasure of examining was about 400 years old and was from Italy. It had brass strings on, and only two or three were broken; it was not kept up to pitch and so was still in rather good condition. It was not pretty, but looked old and brown. Its value? Maybe $3000. But only if you can find a buyer. Its owner would have sold it for perhaps a quarter of that amount. And here you see the big problem. The value of a harp depends on what it will be worth to some buyer; otherwise, you can put the price anywhere you like.

ERARD - ERAT - BROWNE & BUCKWELL - SWEETLAND - NADERMAN - Etc.

Many Erard harps are to be found in old shops. They have a double action and date from around 1860. Some could be as old as 1810 since they were first made at that time, but most extant today are of much later manufacture. Most of them, however they are restored, will be of no value as playing instruments. If you want one to set in a corner and look pretty for a conversation piece, grand, but if you pull it up to pitch, the board will most likely break within a couple of weeks, and the seventy-five dollars you paid for new strings is gone out the window.

Erards may be the most common, but there are also Erat, Browne & Buckwell, Sweetland, Moreley, Degan, and many, many more that are essentially the same thing. You may find little single action harps, also. These are usually much older, and Naderman is the most common. These begin to take on real antique status, and some of them when they are well made and well cared for are charming little instruments. Still, do not attempt to make them playable. Even with a new sound-board installed, (Lyon Healy, by the way, will not attempt work on antique harps.) the mechanism will probably be corroded beyond use. If you have ambition and money, you might try a total restoration, but it is cheaper to buy a big, fancy harp!

Certain individuals from time to time have made one or two harps, and you may encounter some of these. A few harps have been made by a Mr. Laughton, quite a few by a Mr. Aslanian, also Mr. Lindeman. Having no personal experience with these instruments we are not prepared to offer descriptions. Obermeyer in Germany has been turning out ten to fifteen harps a year for about as many years. We know of none owned in this country. Victor Salvi has been making harps in Italy for several years now, and we know of perhaps a half dozen owned in the United Sates.

WATCH FOR DRYING OUT!

Caution is advised on any article made of wood and brought from Europe to America. The climate requires drying the wood to different moisture content and so whether it is a European made harp, or German made Steinway be careful that the climate in your area will not cause trouble with it coming apart. Fortunately, American harps taken to Europe do not dry out but absorb the slight increase in humidity which, if anything, is beneficial.

LOOKING FOR A BARGAIN?

The usual antique harp buyer is really in his heart of hearts looking for a cheap way to get a harp that he can learn to play. We repeat, don't expect to get one of these old harps for $300 and then make a playing instrument out of it. Many have managed to use them to start on and get a certain amount of playing out of them but it is rarely so, and time is constantly working against you. $150 to $300 would be the going price for an antique harp such as the Erard. If a good deal of restoring and gilding, etc., has been done, that might conceivable raise the price to $1000 but still don't count on playing it.

Irish harps, about two and a half feet tall, sold for $400 brand new when the lack of demand caused them to fall from the market. If you find one with a broken neck, it will cost about $250 to have a new neck-column put on. A new board would run about $200. So they are pretty much of a losing proposition unless you must have an Irish harp. There is a small carriage harp that will crop up now and then, less than two feet high. It is shaped more like the standard large harp and has a metal body. These very sturdy little harps may have only a couple dozen strings and not sound like much, but oh how they last! Don't pay more than $75 or $100 if you find one in fair condition.

USED HARPS

A used harp in good condition should be worth about one-half to two-thirds of the same harp new, depending on the age, appearance and condition. Watch out for twisted necks and pulled up sound-boards, but if you can pick it up at a really low price, you could figure on getting the whole thing rebuilt - new neck, new board, action re-riveted and associated work done for $1200 to $1500, and that is for even an extended board. If you can pick up an old harp for less than a thousand and have the work done, you would have a virtually new harp at perhaps considerable savings! The serial number of the harp will give you a good clue to its age. If you want the exact date of manufacture, write to Lyon Healy and they can give you the information.

SERIAL NUMBERS

Lyon Healy started numbering at 500 in 1889, and then after about 200 harps they started over at 100. About 1910 they were numbering harps in the 1000 series. They ticked off about 100 numbers each year so that the first two numbers of the serial number will be within three or four years of the year it was made. At least untill about the depression; then the numbers get a little confused. At anyvrate, if the serial number is 3000 or more it is not considered a really old harp. A good harp is not old until it is past fifty! The Wurlitzer harps were begun about 1915 to 1920, and probably started numbering with 500. They ended in the 1400 series about 1930, so you can figure the approximate age of a Wurlitzer harp. These are the only harps besides Lyon Healy's that the harp factory can and will repair. The costs are the same as for their own harps.

The harp trunk provides excellent protection
for shipping the harp around the world - or changing clothes.

CHAPTER THIRTY-SIX: STORING AND SHIPPING YOUR HARP

We have found that it is rarely advisable to lower the string tension of a harp. The loosening and retightening presents more of a strain on the board than simply leaving the tension even while shipped or stored for a reasonable period of time. If the harp will be stored indefinitely, say in a museum, okay, lower the strings, but otherwise leave them up to pitch. It would be better to rent your harp out, so that it would be played, rather than to leave it with no tension say for two or three years.

TRUCK, TRAIN, OR PLANE

It is most economical to ship a harp by motor frieght, that it, a trucking line. Usually, they are quite fast. Check "Motor Freight" in the yellow pages for a line that will ship it where you want it to go, and who will also pick it up from your house. You may find that you will have to take it to them.

Recently, the rates on air freight have become low enough to compete with the railway, and they are very fast and careful. Check "The Flying Tigers" or other air freight lines listed in the yellow pages.

Railroad express rates have gone up quite high, recently, but they will always pick up and deliver which the truckers may not do, and they do have connections to almost every small town in the United States.

Make sure your trunk is reasonably sound and rigid, and that the door won't fly open. Hasps are important, but locks are not. The cushion blocks should keep the harp far enough from the side of the trunk to give it adequate protection. Label it clearly on both sides, and off it goes.

Trunk repairs can be made right in your own city by a luggage maker or repairman. Check the yellow pages. A locksmith will come out and put a new lock on and replace broken hasps at the same time. New cushion blocks can be ordered from the factory. Specify the exact size you need. These are screwed on from the outside, and you will need an assistant to help you do it.

Harps should always be shipped in a trunk, but if you can do your own moving, a foam rubber mattress or other good cushioning material in the back of a station wagon will provide good protection and much easier handling. Always lay the harp down on the right side so that the action discs are up; otherwise, they may get broken, bent or certainly spoil the regulation.

On an orchestral tour, use the harp trunk for maximum protection - and a good place to store clothes. Try to have the harp unloaded first, so it will have time to adjust its strings to the temperature of the hall.

Sudden extreme changes of temperature may cause the finish to craze or the strings to go false. Avoid them. Never leave the harp and trunk in the sun. And, needless to say, keep it out of the rain and away from radiators and air-conditioners.

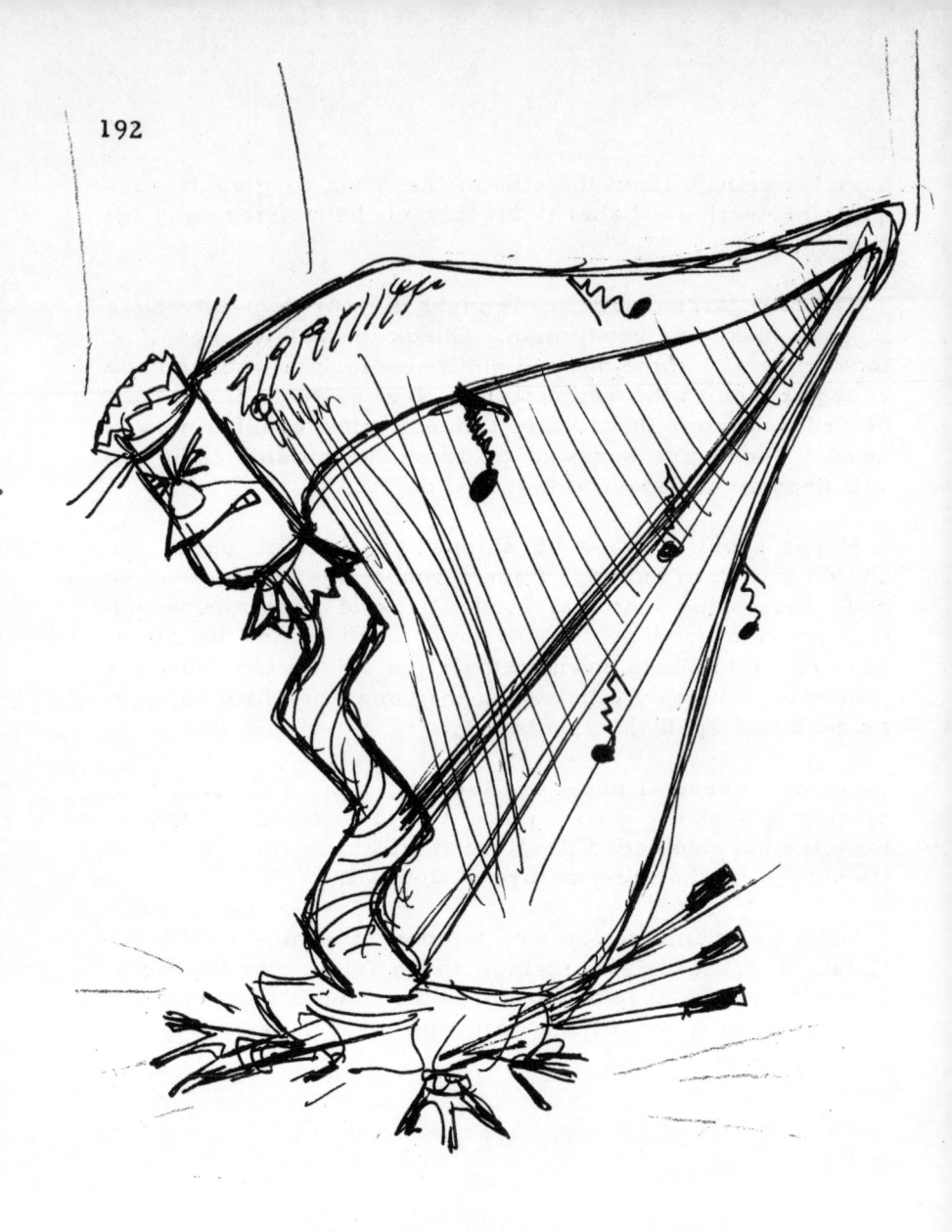

A severe fall may cause hidden damage that
may not show itself for many months!

CHAPTER THIRTY-SEVEN: DAMAGE AND INSURANCE

Some people are lucky and they go through life never breaking a rod, nor a spring nor having anything happen to their harp; but most of us don't. There are a few things we should do in advance, and some we should do after something has happened.

KEEP IT INSURED FOR THE EXACT VALUE

If your harp is dropped or knocked over, even if there is no apparent damage, notify your insurance agent. Give him the date, time and circumstances. What! You don't have an insurance agent! If you never take your harp out of the house and are not a professional, you can have it included in your household insurance. Check with your agent. Otherwise, get sufficient coverage.

Don't over insure, it won't do any good. Don't insure for only half the value, or you may find that they will only pay $500 of the $1000 repair bill. Lyon Healy can provide you with a letter stating the date your harp was made and the replacement cost, assuming that the harp is in good playing condition. This means what you would have to pay for a harp just like yours if you bought it second hand.

DAMAGE MAY SHOW UP LATER

Now you have an insurance agent. You have notified him that something has happened to your harp even though it doesn't seem to be damaged at the moment. Harp damage has a way of showing up a week or two, or even a month or two later. If and when damage does appear, the insurance company will probably send an adjuster out to see it, and these gentlemen will usually call in someone from Lyon Healy to give them an opinion on the damage. It has been our experience that the adjusters are always fair in their judgements and have never slighted a harpist.

With the damage assessed, your harp will go off to the factory to be fixed. It will most likely take two or three months to repair, and Lyon Healy does not provide you with a harp to use in the mean time. If you're lucky you may be able to rent one, and if you're a pro' making your living at harping, the insurance may cover the rent. Try to get this into your policy if it doesn't cost too much.

If you have shipped your harp somewhere, or it has been shipped to you and it arrives with the trunk a mess and apparently damaged, open it on the spot and hold on to the delivery man until he sees it. Get his name and number and anything else you can find out. Don't get mad at him though, he probably didn't do it, and you want him to be on your side. Now call the company who carried it. Report the exact nature of the damage and get them to send out an adjuster to see it. Report it to your own insurance company, too. They will want to know about it since they may have to pay if it was not insured with the shipper.

Note all apparent damage on the bill of lading, the delivery man has you sign.

195

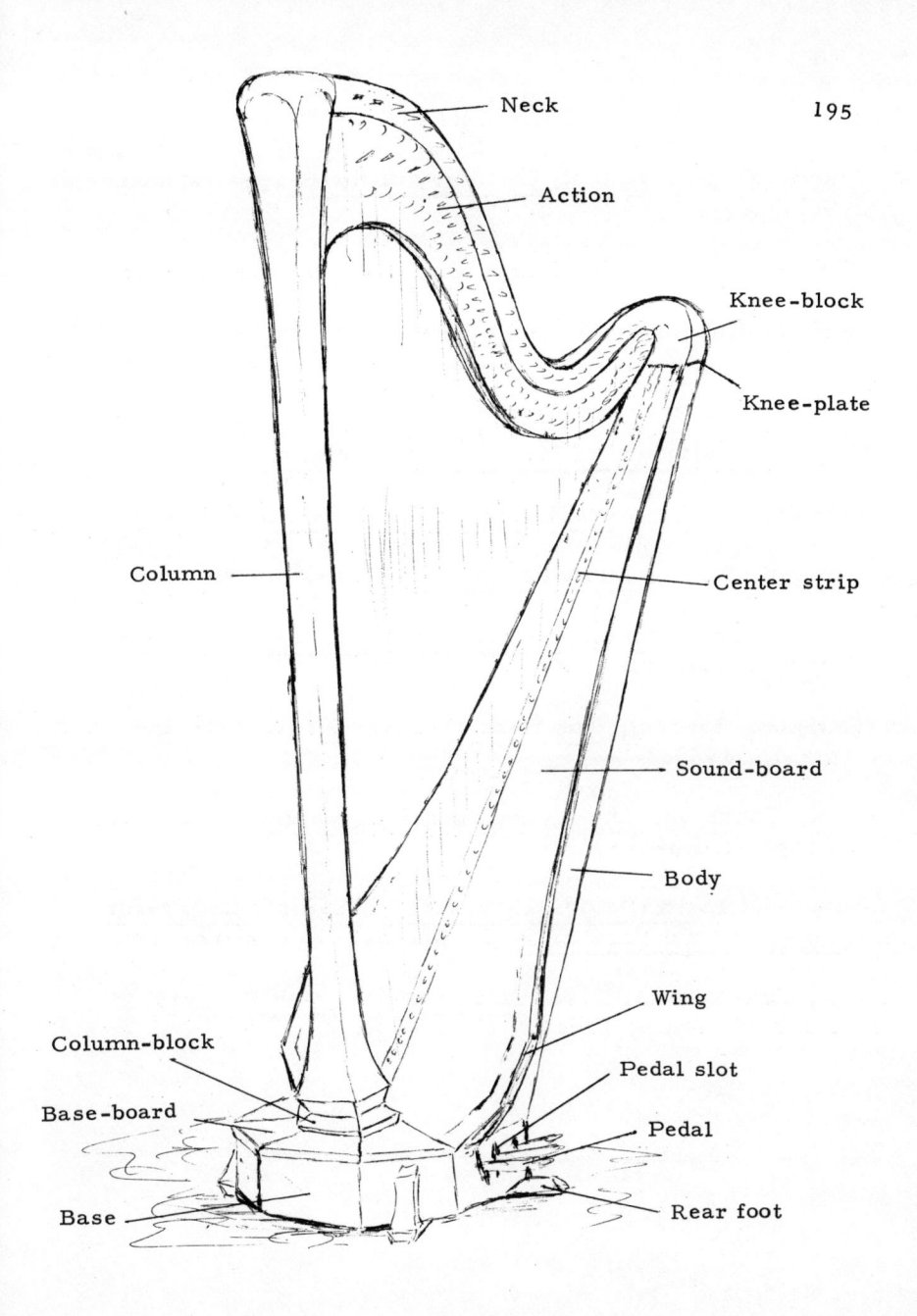

BIBLIOGRAPHY

Flood, W. H. Gratton, The Story of the Harp. London: Scribners, 1905.

Grew, Sidney and Eva Mary, Bach. New York: Collier

Hughes, Rosemary, Haydn. New York: Collier

Schonberg, The Great Pianists. New York: McGraw Hill

Groves, Dictionary of Music and Musicians.

Turner, W. J., Mozart, the Man and his Works.

Trezise, W. J., Miscellaneous Writings. unpub.

Jones, Edw., Musical and Poetical Relicks of the Welsh Bards. London: 1794.

Tournier, Marcel, The Harp. Paris: Henry Lemoine & Co., 1959.

Dart, Thurston, The Interpretation of Music. New York: Harper & Row, 1963.

Gunn, John, An Historical Inquiry Respecting the Performance on the Harp in the Highlands. Edinburgh: 1807.

Fox, Charlotte Milligan, Annals of the Irish Harpers. London: Smith, Elder & Co., 1911.

ABOUT THE AUTHOR

The author's widely varied experience and background make him unusually qualified for the task of writing a definitive work on the harp. His love for the instrument has kept him in close association not only with the harp, but with most of the great harpists of our time and he counts nearly all of the finest performers and teachers of the harp as close acquaintenances and friends.

His years of managing the Lyon Healy harp factory gave him opportunity to bring about some much needed modernization of factory equipment and methods, and to develop the strikingly different style 30, Princess Louise Harp. Although he had made the first Troubadour Harp some years earlier, it was tested thoroughly at the factory and finally worked into production.

His lectures and demonstrations on the care and maintenance of the harp have been given in many of the schools in the United States with prominent harp departments.

Playing the harp, flute and piano equally well, he has appeared as soloist many times on each of these instruments. As flutist, he has appeared as soloist with the Utah Symphony, the Intermountain Little Symphony, the Los Angeles Chamber Symphony, the Columbia University Symphony and in solo recitals. For three years he toured with Reberta Peters as her personal flutist. After seven years "rest" with Lyon Healy, he is now doing the same thing, working concerts with this lovely soprano into his harp schedule.

The author's piano recitals have always included some of his own compositions and usually works of Bach, Debussy and Ravel whom he regards as his teachers. He has played piano recitals among other places at City College in Chicago and Upper Iowa State University.

As harpist, he has played programs and recitals in great number on both the east and west coasts, mostly accompanying himself on the Troubadour harp and singing from his choice collection of folk songs whereby he has amply demonstrated the great versatility and capabilities of this small harp. He has presented many of his own compositions for the pedal harp at the various clinics and lectures he has given. Several of these works have been awarded prizes, including the 1951 Special Award by the Friends of Harvey Gaul for his Chamber Concerto for harp and woodwind quintet.

In Los Angeles, he conducted an orchestra of 110 young people in a youth festival at Hollywood Bowl. About the same time, he wrote and directed a musical play, "Handcarts West," which played a highly successful though limited run as a benefit for the Fort Moore Memorial. Many other small musicals have been written and produced for church groups by the author.

Besides a thorough musical background, he has his B. A. and M. A. degrees from the University of Utah. Mr. Pratt has also pursued an extensive study of clinical and analytical psychology. At Ripon College in Wisconsin, he studied engineering, courtesy of the U. S., Army and was finally sent to the China, Burma, India theatre with the Signal Corps. Later, he studied design and sculpture with the famous American sculptor, Avard Fairbands, and drawing and painting with Albert Dibble. Further work toward his doctorate was done at the Columbia University in New York City.

Years of tuning and repairing pianos earned him the position of Manager of the Piano Repair Shop of Lyon Healy in Chicago, and also further qualified him for research into the problems of repair and regulation of harps.

As a teacher, he was on the staff of the University of Utah for four years and has usually had a number of private students, at one time numbering thirty a week in addition to his regular playing with the Utah Symphony.

An analytical approach to a problem and his firm convictions as to its solution have caused him to write several pamphlets and papers on both the flute and the harp.

His approach to technique on the harp, which is only hinted at in this book, has been gleaned from the various harpists and teachers with whom he has had association, and further developed in the light of history and the early harp virtuosi. His study material is unusual, but extremely logical and well in line with the physical and psychological method of good learning. Already his several "disciples" have demonstrated the soundness of his approach, and the success of its application.

HARP COMPOSITIONS BY THE AUTHOR

Preludes - Book I
  Ariel*
    To a Little Bird
      Ondine
        Homage to Rachmaninoff
          Clouds

Toccata
  Cold Blows the Wind
    Gonna Play on Mah Harp

Castillienne Suite
  Alborada*
    La Gitana Morra
      Granada

Variations on Mozart's Theme for Harp

Sonata in Classic Style*
  Allegro
    Fantasie Quasi Cadenza
      Prestissimo

Charades, harp, flute and string quartet
  Allegro commodo
    Adagio
      Scherzando

Pastoral, solo harp with flute, English horn & strings

Trio in Classic Style, harp, flute and viola

Concerto No. 2 in B Minor, solo harp and orchestra
   Allegro
      Andante Cantabile
         Vivace

Music For Christmas, 3 part women's chorus with harp

Suenos, 3 part women's chorus and 3 part harp ensemble

Blue Ocean, soprano, alto flute, bass clarinet, viola cello and harp

Prelude and Aria, violin and harp

*For troubadour harp or pedal harp

INDEX

Action, 13; arms, 107, 133, 134, 139, 140, 148; blocks, 127, 140; links, 133, 134, 107, 115; plates, 138, 140, 180; removal, 142.
Adjustable nuts, 102-107, 109, 114.
American Harp Society, 43, 46, 65.
Amplified harp, 67.
Antique harps, 185.
Appraisal, 193.
Auditions, 35, 71.

Bach, J. S., 24, 44, 67.
Back plate screw, 114-116.
Back plate washer, 117, 138, 148.
Base, 89, 151; bolts, 91, 152; bushings, 152, 170.
Base-board, 13, 169.
Bass discs, 106.
Beats, 96.
Beethoven, 26, 43, 64.
Bench, 174.
Blind harpists, 34.
Blocks, body, 11, 168; glue, 151, 175; knee, 13, 37, 137; pedal, 121.
Bluth, Donald, 2.
Board, see sound-board.
Bochsa, 17, 29, 51.
Body, 12, 13, 168; blocks, 12, 168; panels, 13, 168; shell, 12; strips, 12.
Bridge (sub-center-strip), 166
Broken, pedal rods, 125-128; necks, 156; screws, 134; springs, 119-123; sound-boards, 160-167.
Buttons, 166.

Caps, pedal, 91, 114.
Cello, 162.
Celluloid tubes, 106.
Center strip, 115.
Chalifoux, Alice, 2.
Checks, 162, 191.
Chopin, 31, 43.
Chromatic harp, 7, 20, 29, 60.
Clavier, 20, 24, 28, 64.
Cleaning, 180; action, 180; finish, 180; gold, 180.
Clicks, 115, 137, 138.
Column, 5, 13, 172, 173; carving, 172; block, 169; gilding, 181.
Composer, 34, 39, 45, 46, 60-62, 66.
Conductor, 40, 69-73.
Coupler, pedal rod, upper, 140; lower, 106, 121, 126, 127; screw, 108, 121.
Covers, 182.
Cracks, 156, 162.
Critics, 64-67.

Crown, 173.
Cushion blocks, 15, 190.

Damage, 193.
Debussy, 60.
deVolt, Artiss, 28.
Diagonal back plate, 143.
Disassembly, action, 142, 144; harp, 169.
Disc, 9, 101, 105, 107, 148; broken, send for replacement; open, 105; oversize, 111; pins, 158, 159.
Double action harp, 7, 9, 29, 31.
Double harp (see chrom. harp), 20.
Durkee, George, 9.

Egyptian harp, 5. 6.
Elbow, see knee block.
Erard harp, 9, 185, 187.
Erard, Sebastian, 7.
Etudes for the harp, 55.
Extended sound-board, 9, 164.
Eyelets, 66.

Feet, 153.
Felt, pedal, 89, 100, 106; stuffing, 120, 126, 127, 145.
Finish, 13, 168, 180; craze, 191; checks, 162; touch-up, 169, 181, 183.
Frozen pedals, 133- 135.

Gluck, 19.

Glue, 115, 152, 166, 172, 177-181; blocks, 151, 175; failure, 157, 179; strips, 165.
Gold leaf, 170, 181.
Grandjany, Marcel, 2.
Guarantee, 3, 144, 164.
Guitar, 9, 67.

Handel, 19.
Hanon, 50, 56.
Hasp, 190.
Hasselmans, 17, 30.
Harmonics, 46.
Harp, chromatic, 7; construction, 12; etudes, 55, 56; European, 19, 65, 185, 186; history, 5, 17; in the orchestra, 19, 34, 70, 72; Irish, 18, 187; music, 17-32, 36, 42, 64; names of the parts, see illustrations on pages, 79, 90, 103, 107, 117, 121, 140, 147, 195; pedals, 60, 126, 145; placement in orchestra, 70; production, 15, 65; technique, 19, 28, 31, 34, 50, 55, 60; Troubadour, 9, 86.
Harpoons, 2, also see list of illustrations.
Harpsichord, 26, 64, 177.
History, 5, 17.
Hochbrucker, 7, 17, 20.

Inserts, rear shoe, 154.
Insurance, 193; appraisal, 193.

Ireland, 7, 18, 19.
Irish harp, see harp.
Jazz, 137.
Jones, Edward, 29.

Kahootch, 145.
Knee block, 13, 37, 117; cracked, 157; open joint, 157.
Knee plate, 117.
Krumpholz, 17, 21, 29.

LaBarre, Theo., 17, 30.
Lacquer, 13, 180.
Links (action), 107, 115, 137, 148.
Liszt, 30, 64.
Locks, 190.
Loose arms on spindle, 139.
Lute, 9, 101.
Lyon Healy, 9, 12, 15, 37, 65, 125, 139, 145, 193.

Mahler, 61.
Main action, 137, 140.
Malone, Eileen, 2.
Maple, 177.
Mendelssohn, 24, 44.
Mexico, 19.
Monteverde, 19/
Mormon Tabernacle, 178.
Movers, harp, 39, 190.
Mozart, L., 20.
Mozart, W., 27, 28.
Music, harp, 17-32, 36, 42, 55, 64.

Naderman, 17, 21, 29, 186.
Names of parts, see harp.
Neck, 13, 107, 156-159; broken, 156; cracks, 157; studs, 107, 143; twisted, 156, 158.
Notation, 47.
Nuts, adjustable, 102-105, 107, 114; stationary, 105, 110, 116, 142.
Nylon strings, 76.

Obermeyer, 186.
Oil, 115, 133, 134, 148.
Oiling, 115, 122, 126, 133, 134, 145, 148, 149.
Open discs, 105, 139.
Orchestral harpist, 34-40.
Orchestral music, 36.
Overhauling, see re-rivet, neck, sound-board.
Over motion, 89, 106, 128.
Oversize discs, 111.

Panels, back, 168; side, 13, 168.
Paraguay, 19.
Paris Concervatoire, 30.
Parish-Alvars, 17, 29, 31, 65.
Pedal, 60; assembly, 15, 126, 145; bar, 106, 108, 121, 126, 138, 145; block, 121, 145; brass, 90; caps, 91, 114; felt, 89, 100, 105, 106; foam rubber, 89; frozen, 133-135; fulcrum, 121, 145; rod couplers, 106, 121, 126, 127, 140, 145; rod coupler

screw, 108, 121, 138; rod tubes, 9, 13, 126; rods, 9, 100, 106, 115, 125-128, 140; slots, 151; wrapping, see felt.
Pegs, sound-board, 165, see eyelets; tuning, see tuning pins.
Piano, 26, 30, 49, 60, 67, 100, 177.
Plates, 138, 140, 180; back, 117; cleaning, 180; cleaning, 180; front, 147; knee, 117.
Polish, 180.
Posse, Wm., 17, 43, 64.
Practice, 40, 50.
Primitive harps, 5, 6, 19.
Princess Louise, style 30, 9, 127, 168, 172, 183.
Programming, 45, 57.
Pulled-up sound-board, 101, 104, 138, 164, 166.

Regulation, 3, 15, 86, 89, 100-112; adjustable nut, 102-107; disc, 103-108; pedal rod, 89, 106; pitch, 100.
Removing the action, 142.
Renie, Henrietta, 17, 31.
Repairs, 194.
Replacing, the neck, 156-159; action, 142; board, 160-167.
Re-rivet, 115, 133, 137.
Ribs, 166; spruce, 11.
Risers, 70.
Rivet, 107, 133.
Rods, pedal, 100, 125-128; coupler, 106, 121, 126, 127, 140, 145; tubes, 9, 13, 126.
Rossini, 44.

Salvi, 186.
Salzedo, 2, 46.
Salzedo model harp, 172.
Scales, 61.
Scarlatti, A., 20, 44.
Schumann, 43.
Schmidt, 51.
Screws, 178; adjustable-nut, 107; back-plate, 114-117; broken, 116, 134; column, 169; crown, 114; disc, 107; handle, 114; pedal-cap, 114; pedal-rod-coupler, 108.
Shipping, 190.
Shoes, 153, 154; front, 114 inserts, 154; rear, 114.
Side-strips, 165, 166.
Sight-reading, 34, 62, 71.
Single-action harp, 29.
Single-pin disc, 111, 112.
Slots, pedal, 151.
Sound-board, 13, 87, 160-167; broken, 164, 165; cracked or checked, 162, 165; pegs, 165; pulled-up, 101, 104, 105, 138, 164, 166; replacement, 164, 167.
Spindle, 139, 140; loose arm, 139.
Springs, 119-123; back-plate, 114-116; pedal, 119-123;

studs, 138.
Spruce, 11, 177.
Squeaks, 145, 146.
Stand, music, 174.
Stationary-nut, 79, 105, 110, 116; washer, 79, 116, 158.
Steinway, 67, 186.
Storing, 190.
Stirrups, 138.
Strings, 15, 69, 75, 114, 162, 190; centering, 102, 109; color, 84; false, 75; guaging, 84; gut, 75; knot, 78; length, 101, 167; nylon, 76; stringing, 75-84; wire, 80, 81, 110, 158.
Studs, pedal-spring, 120-123, 138; neck, 117.

Talber, three hand effect, 30.
Teaching, 49-53.
Temperment, 15, 94.
Thomas, John, 28.
Toch, Ernst, 43.
Trade-in, 188; also check with Lyon Healy
Transcriptions, 31, 57, 64.
Trezise, Wm., 2.
Trnecek, 17, 43.
Troubadours, 5.
Troubadour Harp, 9, 86.
Trucking, 190.
Trunks, 15, 190; cushion blocks, 15, 190; hasps, 191; locks, 191. repairs, 191.

Tuning, 37, 60, 69, 94-99.
Tuning key, 130.
Tuning-pins, 79, 117, 130, 131.

Used harps, 187, see antique harps.

Veneers, body, see body shell; checks, 162; cracks, 156, 162; neck, 13, 156; soundboard, 160, 162, 164.
Viol, 19.
Violin, 161, 177.

Wagner, R., 40, 61, 71.
Washers, back-plate, 117; neck-stud, 117; stationary-nut, 79, 158.
Wings, 13; bolt, 164.
Wood, 13, 101, 115, 118, 160-162, 177-181, 186.
Wurlitzer, 12, 65, 120.

Zabaleta, N., 24.
Zabel, A., 17, 43.